Saturday Night at Moody's Diner

Even More Stories by Tim Sample

Also by Tim Sample

Illustrator

How to Talk Yankee (Gerald Lewis)
Stories Told in the Kitchen (Kendall Morse)

Audio

Down East Stand-Up
How to Talk Yankee (with Bob Bryan)
Back in Spite of Popular Demand
Snappy Answers
Pumping Irony
The Sun Dog (Stephen King)

Video

Best of Tim Sample
Postcards from Maine
Tourist Huntin' in Maine
Maine Humor Behind the Barn
Tim Sample on a Roll

Saturday Night at Moody's Diner

Even More Stories

Written and Illustrated
by Tim Sample

Down East Books
Camden, Maine

Second Edition
ISBN 0-89272-385-8

Portions of this book are derived from material originally recorded on *Downeast Standup, How to Talk Yankee,* and *Back in Spite of Popular Demand,* produced and distributed by Bert & I Records, Ipswich, Massachusetts. The author and publisher gratefully acknowledge the use of this material.

Designed on Crummett Mountain by Edith Allard

Printed and bound at Capital City Press, Montpelier, Vt.

10 9 8 7 6 5 4 3 2

Library of Congress Cataloging-in-Publication Data
Sample, Tim.
Saturday night at Moody's Diner, and other stories / written and illustrated by Tim Sample.
p. cm.
ISBN 0-89272-385-8 (pbk.)
1. Maine—Social life and customs—Humor. 2. American wit and humor—Maine. I. Title.
F19.6.S27 1996
974.1—dc20 96-2239
CIP

Down East Books
P.O. Box 679
Camden, ME 04843
207-594-9544

Contents

For Ken and Julia Bergquist

I'd like to thank the following individuals who have contributed greatly to my understanding and appreciation of life in general and Down East humor in particular: Capt. Kendall Morse, Joe Perham, Rev. Robert Bryan, Marshall J. Dodge III, my uncle "Stevie" Graham, Noel Paul Stookey, Robert McCloskey, Steve and Tabby King, and last, but not least, Edith Allard.

-FLASH-

Tim Sample Saves America!

By Stephen King

Okay. Okay.

So Tim didn't save America.

Exactly.

But he *has* been responsible for saving a part of America, an *important* part, and if you'll lend me your ear for just a few minutes before turning it (your ear, that is) over to Mr. Sample, I think I can make you understand what I mean. And by the way, up in these parts, *ear* rhymes with the girl's name *Leah.* If you can get that straight and keep that straight, you've come a fair way toward understanding Maine humor. Deah.

As to how Tim Sample has saved and continues to save America with each book and each gig (even with his amusing answering machine tapes), well, consider this: every six months or so, some self-appointed guardian of the English language, American style, will proclaim our native dialects either dead or on life support systems. These self-appointed Jeremiahs (William Safire and William Safire wannabes, you know the type) solemnly assure us that in another six months, a year at best, we're all going to sound pretty much alike, all the guys like Tom Brokaw and all the gals like Katie Couric. Dialect and regionalism, they mourn, have been murdered. And what planted the dagger in the heart of linguistic diversity? TV, of course. Same old bad guy.

The only problem with the theory is that it's nonsense. People continue to reflect the areas from which they come both in their dialects and in their yarns; different parts of the country have their own kinds of humor, as well. It's a point-of-view thing, and it's what Tim Sample has always celebrated in his live shows, his writing, and his funky drawings.

He's a funny guy, you'll get no argument from me on that score, but no more a comedian than Mark Twain or Artemus Ward. Like them, Timmy (that's what I always call him, the way folks from up our way are apt to call their friends "dearie") isn't acting; he's just talking in a kind of heightened and gifted way, as folks do when they're passing on valuable tales about the human condition. The fact that most such tales happen to be funny is just a little extra added treat, like a dollop of whipped cream on your slice of pumpkin pie.

I first learned the Maine way of speaking—which outsiders sometimes label "Maine wit" or "Down East wit"—from my grandfather, Guy Pillsbury. Once, when I was five or six, and chattering away to him about something or other I considered vitally important, Daddy Guy leaned forward in his rocking chair, fixed me with his bleary left eye (it had been wounded somehow in a logging accident, and the bottom hung loose and red—a fascinating if somewhat dreadful sight for a small boy), and said: "Teachin' you to talk might've been a bad idear, Stevie—ev'ry time you open your mouth, all your guts fall out."

Another time, while watching *Ted Mack's Amateur Hour* on TV, Daddy Guy and I observed a fellow who could play "Tangerine" on two trumpets at the same time, one jutting from each corner of his mouth. "Fella that musical could maybe blow three-part harmony, if his butt was talented," Daddy Guy remarked, and I laughed for the rest of the day. (That one, in fact, has amused me for the rest of my *life*.) The Maine vernacular is dry, ironic without being sarcastic, exactly, and generally brief. What's funny, more often than not, is in what is left out . . . as in the story of the fellow who pulls up to a general store somewhere out in East Overshoe and asks the guy on the porch if it matters which road he takes to Vassalboro. "Not to me, it don't," the guy on the porch replies serenely.

Although Tim Sample reveres Marshall Dodge as the man who more or less perfected the Maine dialect and reinvented Maine humor, I'd have to say that I prefer Tim's take on it. Marshall was witty and insightful (as is the wonderful Joe Perham), but Tim Sample is a *storyteller*, one who seems to remember every funny thing he's ever seen on the stage of Maine life, as well as every funny anecdote he has ever overheard. He is, in fact, a keeper of his region's unique way of saying and seeing, the sort of man who assures us that, when it comes to the American idiom, any reports of death are very much premature.

Let's not get heavy, though—most of this is just pure fun . . . and not just for Down Easters, either. You don't have to have ever stepped a foot inside of Moody's Diner to know exactly what Tim is talking about; you've probably got a Moody's within driving distance of your own home town . . . or did when you were growing up. And while you may never have had a Hubert in the house (or the barn), you will still recognize him, I think. He's a type, and one that Tim has drawn true.

So Tim has done three great things in his career, in typically modest Down East fashion: he has accurately set down the stories and voices of his home place, he has made them universal, and he has captured our own unique version of humorous storytelling.

I remember something that happened when I was a kid—just after yet another tiresome visit from Mrs. Jolley, from up the road (in Maine, chummy, *road* most commonly rhymes with *mud*). On that particular day Mrs. Jolley had boasted to my mother that, although she had been born in Boston, she had lived in Maine for sixty years without ever leaving. Not even to go "o'er New Ham'shire," she said. When she was gone, Daddy Guy beckoned me over to his rocker with one long, arthritis-twisted finger. His bad eye drooped, but his mouth twisted up on one side. Although this made him look like he was having a stroke, I had learned this actually meant he was about to say something funny or something wise. Often, it seemed to me, there was no difference.

"She say she'd been here sixty years, Stevie?" Daddy Guy asked. When I nodded, he pointed into the kitchen. "See that stove?" I nodded again. "If your cat 'us to have kittens in there, would you call 'em biscuits?" I shook my head and Daddy Guy sat back in his rocking chair, nodding and chuffing his version of laughter. I laughed with him . . . but doubtfully. I wasn't sure I got it, which is often the case with Maine humor. I laughed harder when I read it in this marvelous showcase of Tim Sample's wit and talent and good-heartedness.

No, I guess Timmy didn't exactly save all of America with this book . . . but I think maybe he saved a piece of it, just the same.

Stick your nose on in here, chummy, turn a few pages, and see if you don't agree.

About Maine Humor

About Maine Humor

For quite a few years now, I've spent a fair amount of my spare time performin' and recordin' this "Maine Humor." I guess you'd say it comes pretty natural to me seein' as how I was born and raised here.* But lately I've noticed from the questions people ask that there seems to be some confusion as to what *exactly* this Maine Humor really is. Folks wonder, for instance, if it is humor *from* Maine, humor *about* Maine, humor *poking fun* at Maine, or maybe some combination of it all. Well, of course, I can't claim to clear up the issue entirely, but I believe I might be able to shed a little light on the subject for you.

First off, it will help if you understand a few things about Maine in general, like the fact that we've only got three categories of folks livin' here. Primarily, of course, there are Natives, that select group of individuals fortunate enough to have actually been born here in the Pine Tree State.

*All proper credentials documentin' this assertion are available from the Publisher.

NATIVE
EMERGENCY HEATING WITH ANTIQUES
TRANSPLANT
FROM AWAY

The second category is made up of folks who are frequently referred to by the Natives as being From Away (Portsmouth, New Hampshire, to Antarctica and all points in between).

The third group is commonly known as Transplants, folks who originally came From Away and then decided to settle down here permanently.

You've got to understand right from the start that there's nothing wrong with belonging to any of these categories. Where the real trouble begins is when folks that ought to be in one category, try to sneak over into another one. I'll tell you an example of what I'm talkin' about.

My next door neighbor, Blinky Pinkham, lives in the next trailer over from mine (about four miles down the road). Most folks hereabouts just assume that Blinky is a Native, especially since he's ninety-seven years old and has been livin' out on this road as long as anybody can remember. But I happen to know the truth about Blinky. He was originally born over to Keene, New Hampshire, and he was at least six months old before he ever set foot in the state of Maine.

Blinky was over to my place for a visit a while back, and the conversation got around to the subject of his Native status.

"To be real truthful," he says, "I'm not a Native Mainer."

"I know that, Blinky," says I.

A little bit defensive at this point, Blinky shot back, "On the other hand, Mother and I have four grown children, all of 'em born and raised right in this town. I guess you'd have to call *them* Natives."

"Well, Blinky," I replied, "You can call 'em anythin' you've a mind to, but I'll tell you this, if my cat was to have kittens in the oven, I wouldn't necessarily call 'em biscuits!"

Now, it would be easy to get the impression from that kind of remark that Mainers are hostile towards outsiders, but

nothin' could be further from the truth. The fact is that the average Native Mainer is probably more genuinely tolerant of the diverse eccentricities of human nature than anybody on the face of the earth. What we won't stand for, however, is the attitude, either stated or implied, that being From Away somehow makes the newcomer superior to the Native. Just about anyone, from just about anywhere, can survive, even do pretty well, in Maine so long as they bear in mind that any true Native worth his salt has a finely developed natural instinct for deflating overblown egos if they should happen to stray within range.

Saturday Night at Moody's Diner

Saturday Night at Moody's Diner

If you plan to visit Maine in the summertime, or if you're a Native and you expect some out-of-state friends or relatives to drop by for a visit, I've got some good advice for you. The summer just won't be complete without a visit to some of our fine restaurants.

Now, as you probably know, Maine is blessed with a whole raft* of dining establishments, many of which are world-renowned for their food and atmosphere. You can enjoy spectacular sunset vistas of the rockbound shoreline while feasting on platters of lobsters, steamed clams, and fresh native corn-on-the-cob. Or perhaps you prefer a secluded mountain hide-away with that continental-type cuisine. But I can tell you right now that if you really want the ultimate dinin' experience in the Pine Tree State, you've got but one choice.

*Raft: (noun) an extremely large quantity

The place I'm referrin' to is located smack dag in the middle of Route One, gift shop capital of the universe. You pull onto Route One when you cross the Maine border in Kittery, and before you've rolled up a hundred miles you will be exposed to a greater collection of gift shops and factory outlets than most folks ever see in two lifetimes. You will find every item you ever dreamed of, and a lot of stuff you had no idea you needed until you saw it.

But we're talkin' about restaurants here, not gift shops. You keep drivin' through Wiscasset, past Damariscotta, and you'll begin to approach the town of Waldoboro. Now, Waldoboro ain't that big of a town, so you've got to keep your eyes peeled, but I'll tell you how you know you're gettin' close. When you start comin' into Waldoboro you'll find yourself headin' down this wicked* steep hill. I'm not referrin' to just a dip in the road. This hill is so steep that, dependin' on how good your brakes are, you start feelin' kind of religious about halfway down. You might even start feeling around on the dashboard for a handful of Jimmy Swaggart tapes. And what makes that hill so frightenin' in the summertime is that there is a little stream at the foot of it, and most of the time there's just enough fog comin' off that stream so you can't see the end of the hill.

*Wicked: (adverb) very

Well, just trust me. If you keep on goin' you'll eventually level off and start headin' up the other side. Keep a sharp lookout and you'll see the sign just up ahead on the right, loomin' out of the fog as you approach. It's a great big orange sign with neon letters that just says MOODY'S DINER.

When you see that sign you'll know you've arrived at the finest restaurant in the state of Maine. As soon as you pull into the parkin' lot you'll feel right at home, because Moody's ain't one of them huge rambling places that you could get lost in. As a matter of fact, the buildin' is kind of long and narrow, just like your trailer. It even has a little wooden entryway like you have on your trailer, with a pair of them little ceramic cats grabbin' onto the outside of it like they were chasin' each other up to the roof. They've even got a couple of them exploded tires out front, just like you've got on the lawn in front of your trailer. You know the kind I mean. It's a regular tire, still mounted on the rim, but it's exploded inside out with the edges cut into jagged points, so it looks like Jughead's hat in the comics.

When you come in through the door at Moody's you have to take a sharp right or left turn (like I said, it's kind of long and narrow) and you set yourself down at one of them little handmade plywood booths. Them booths are built for intimate dinin'. In fact, you can't set directly across from each other or your knees are apt to bump. Once you get comfortable you'll notice that each booth has its own private little jukebox, the type where you get to hear the song that the truck driver who sat there before you wanted to hear. They've got all the classic tunes too, like *How can I miss you when you won't go away* and *How come you believed me when I told you that I loved you when you know I've been a liar all my life*. As a matter of fact, that last song is what Mother and I call Our Song.

And, of course, they have all the fine accessories you'd

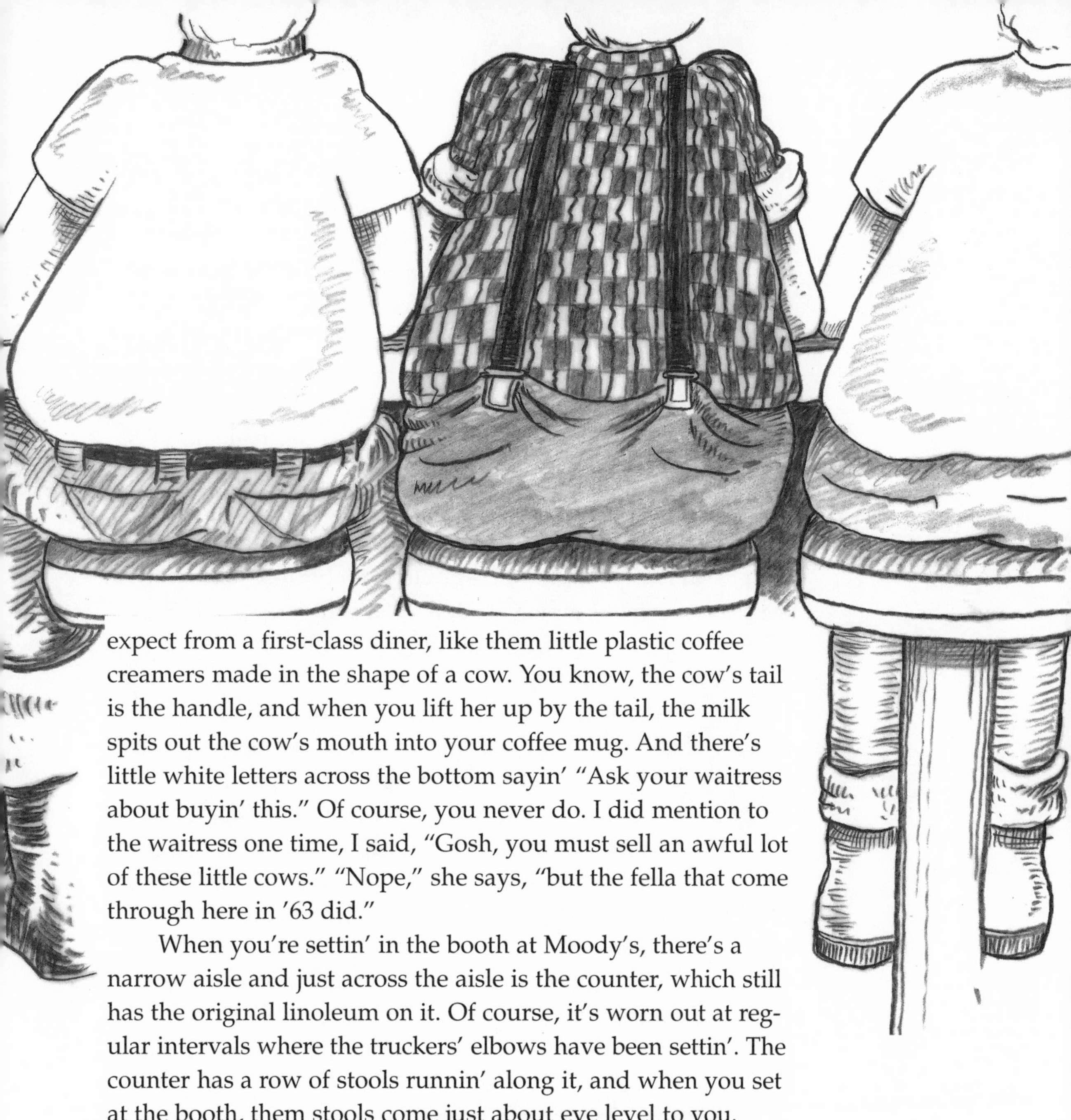

expect from a first-class diner, like them little plastic coffee creamers made in the shape of a cow. You know, the cow's tail is the handle, and when you lift her up by the tail, the milk spits out the cow's mouth into your coffee mug. And there's little white letters across the bottom sayin' "Ask your waitress about buyin' this." Of course, you never do. I did mention to the waitress one time, I said, "Gosh, you must sell an awful lot of these little cows." "Nope," she says, "but the fella that come through here in '63 did."

When you're settin' in the booth at Moody's, there's a narrow aisle and just across the aisle is the counter, which still has the original linoleum on it. Of course, it's worn out at regular intervals where the truckers' elbows have been settin'. The counter has a row of stools runnin' along it, and when you set at the booth, them stools come just about eye level to you. You'll have to remember that part, it's pertinent to the story.

Whenever Mother and I make plans to go to Moody's Diner, we always do it on a Saturday night. On Saturdays

Moody's has a special which can't be beat for pure downright value anywhere in the state of Maine. It's a dinner special featuring all you can eat—homemade baked beans.

But you get a lot more for your money than just the beans. Oh, sure, they give you a good big charge* of beans to start off with, but there's also a man-sized paper cup of cole slaw made with real Miracle Whip, there's a little side plate with two of them nice big puffy homemade rolls steamin' hot right out of the microwave. And settin' alongside them rolls is one small square of what I believe to be the hardest butter on the East Coast of the United States. That butter is so hard that I'll wager you could hoist a pat of it up on the end of your knife, lean back, and drive that butter right through the roll, the plate, the table, and everythin' else, and you wouldn't so much as put a scratch in the butter.

Then on your plate next to the beans you get two of them big bright red hot dogs. Not just pinkish lookin', you understand. I'm talkin' about the bright red kind that looks like the flares the truck drivers keep under their seats in case of emergency. Now, personally, I don't care for them hot dogs as far as eatin' em goes, but I'll always have the waitress pack 'em up for me after the meal so I can take 'em home with me. I swear there's nothin' finer than them hot dogs when you're deep trollin' for salmon. You can lace a couple of number three hooks into 'em and they'll take two or three good strikes and still hang onto the hook.

Now, Moody's is not only known for its value but its atmosphere as well. To give you some idea, I want to tell you of an incident that happened to us on this one particular Saturday night at Moody's. Mother and I had just settled in for our first round of beans when we heard a pickup truck pull in out front. Now you have to understand that Moody's is located

*Charge: (noun) a large serving

just a few miles down the road from the town of Rockland, Maine, and as anyone can tell you, Rockland has been known for generations as a great fishin' village. Nowadays, of course, the fishin' ain't as great as it once was, but just the same there's still some able-bodied seamen who'll slip out for a week or two at a stretch, for a share of the catch. And whether they make much money or not, there's two things that remain constant. They tend to work up a powerful appetite, and they tend to get pretty gamy.* As a matter of fact, I've seen some of them so gamy when they walked in the door at Moody's that they set off the smoke detector.

*Gamy: (adjective) foul smelling

Well, on this particular night, that pickup pulled into the parkin' lot, and we heard these three fellas get out. They stomped up the steps and opened the entryway door. There happened to be a bit of a tailwind behind 'em that evening and there was no question in anyone's mind that these boys was fishermen. And big ones too, I might add. I'd say that the smallest one of the three would dress out at close to 250 pounds. And from the way they stormed up to the counter I would say they were mighty hungry too.

As luck would have it, they decided to set on the three stools directly opposite me and Mother. And they'd barely plunked down on them stools, before they were bailin' them beans to 'em at a rate that would strain the imagination of most folks. I wasn't keepin' exact count, but I'd say they were scarfin' down three or four plateloads of them beans to our one. I've never seen the like of it.

Now as everyone knows, there is an inevitable physiological consequence which accompanies the consumption of a large quantity of this particular vegetable. And the effect is exacerbated when they are consumed in an enclosed environment. Not that there is anythin' wrong with it, you understand. That's just the way folks are constructed, and have been since the dawn of time, for all we know. But down through the centuries, hundreds of various techniques have been devised to deal with this potentially embarrassing problem. Now, I haven't the time or the inclination to go into all the details at this point. However, if you think about it, I believe you'll agree that virtually all of these diverse techniques for alleviatin' the excess buildup in our system would fall into one of two general categories.

Category One (generally preferred by professional people) is a technique whereby you allow this buildup to escape in such a manner that it's virtually impossible to determine that it has escaped at all. At least for a few minutes. At which point it is equally impossible to correctly affix blame.

Category Two on the other hand (generally preferred by sportsmen) is what I simply refer to as the "Let 'er Rip" approach.

Well, let me put it to you this way. There was no question in my mind that these fellas were sportsmen. The largest one of 'em, who was seated to Mother's immediate left, let go with what I would conservatively estimate to be a forty-eight-second fart that darned near blew the doors off that diner.

I'll tell you, chummy, it was pure pandemonium in that diner. There were two elderly ladies up at one end, and their teacups jumped about six inches off the table. There were a half dozen anti-nuclear types down at the other end, and they immediately leaped under the table, figurin' Wiscasset had finally blowed up. There was even a busload of school kids comin' back from an outin' at summer camp, and the bus pulled into the parkin' lot thinkin' they had a blowout in one of the tires. It seemed as though all creation was bustin' loose.

HOW DARE YOU!?

Of course, them boys just kept bailin' them beans to 'em just like nothin' ever happened. Everybody started lookin' up our way, Mother was gettin' kind of embarrassed at all the publicity, and frankly I felt called upon to make some sort of rebuttal. Not that I liked the idea, you understand, but Mother's honor was involved. So I stood up and tapped this fella on the shoulder. He just kept on bailin' beans. I tapped a little harder. Still no response. Finally I gathered up all my nerve and yelled at the top of my lungs, "HOW DARE YOU??!!!"

He turned around and gave me a blank stare. Seeing that I had his attention, I pressed on. "How dare you," I said, "set there on that stool and do such a thing before my wife here?" I was pointin' toward Mother as I said it. He put down his fork, turned around slowly, and looked at Mother. Then he turned back to me and said, "Gosh, if I'da knowed it was her turn, I'da let her go first."

So if you're ever steering a course for Down East Maine and you chance to find yourself in Waldoboro on a Saturday night, you owe it to yourself to check out Moody's Diner. The food is second to none, the atmosphere is cozy, and of course the entertainment runs twenty-four hours a day.

Unc's Store

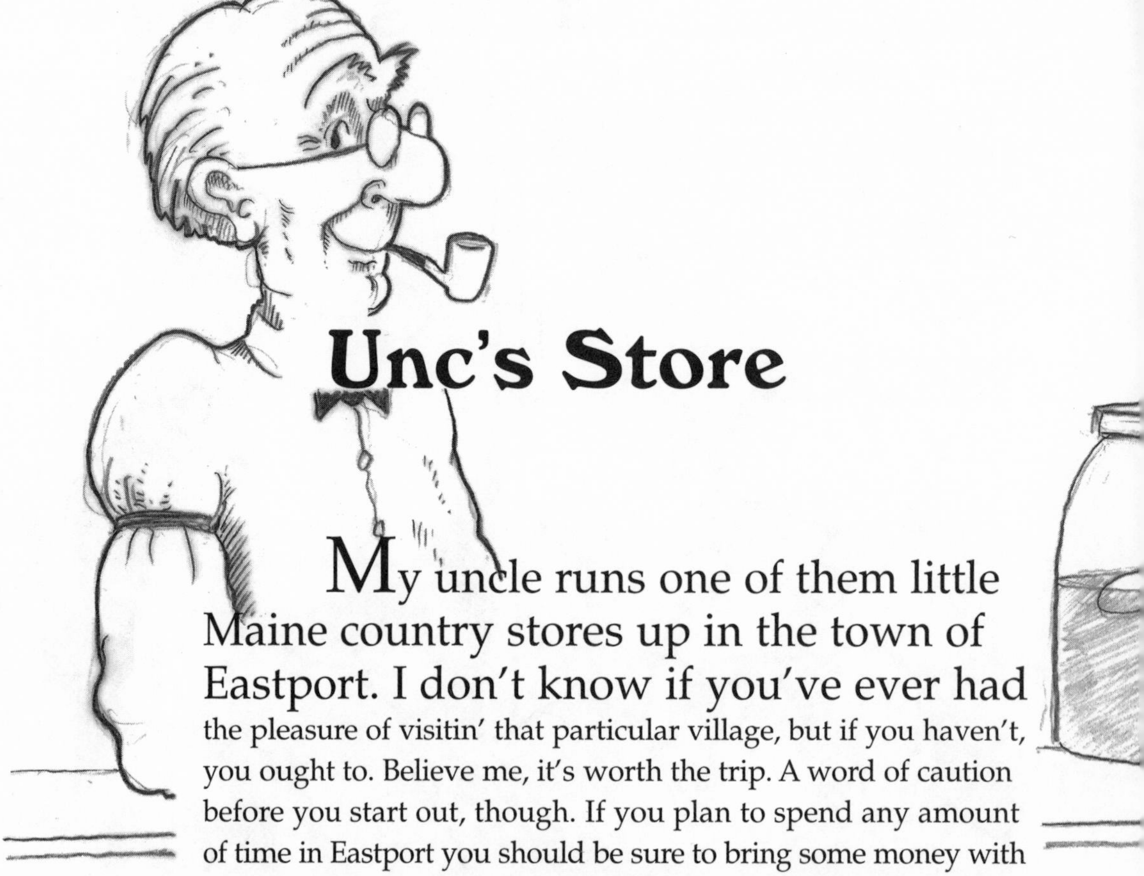

Unc's Store

My uncle runs one of them little Maine country stores up in the town of Eastport. I don't know if you've ever had the pleasure of visitin' that particular village, but if you haven't, you ought to. Believe me, it's worth the trip. A word of caution before you start out, though. If you plan to spend any amount of time in Eastport you should be sure to bring some money with you, because you ain't apt to find any growin' wild up that way.

The town of Eastport has fallen on some hard times since the big economic boom around the turn of the century. It's still one of the loveliest spots in the state, but as Unc always says, "If you could buy a Greyhound bus ticket with a food stamp, we'd all be gone outta here."

Of course, Unc has a reputation for sayin' that type of thing. It's not that he's mean or anythin'. You just get a certain viewpoint on life after runnin' one of them stores as long as he has. It's a nice little place just like a hundred others you're apt to encounter on Maine's back roads. Just a gray clapboard buildin'

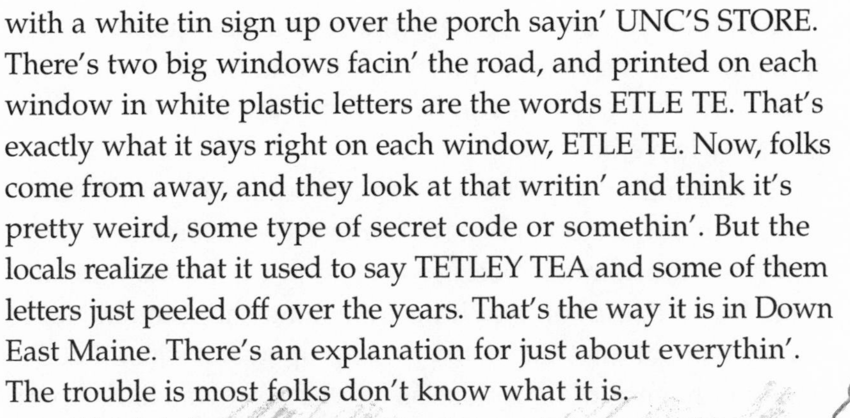

with a white tin sign up over the porch sayin' UNC'S STORE. There's two big windows facin' the road, and printed on each window in white plastic letters are the words ETLE TE. That's exactly what it says right on each window, ETLE TE. Now, folks come from away, and they look at that writin' and think it's pretty weird, some type of secret code or somethin'. But the locals realize that it used to say TETLEY TEA and some of them letters just peeled off over the years. That's the way it is in Down East Maine. There's an explanation for just about everythin'. The trouble is most folks don't know what it is.

Which brings me to another interestin' aspect of life in

Maine. When you come up here and start askin' questions among the Natives, you're pretty apt to find that it's not so much what they say that you have to pay attention to, it's what they leave out.

I remember this particular day one summer I was workin' for Unc up at the store. I believe it must have been about three o'clock in the afternoon, because we had just got done watchin' *As the World Twirled* on that little TV behind the counter. Not that we were all that interested in soap operas, it's just that you don't have a lot of options as to what you watch. Eastport, you see, ain't "cable ready." We only get two stations that come in any good. We get one of the Bangor stations, the one with all the old movies and the Slim Whitman record advertisements. I've always wondered how Slim Whitman sold forty million records before I'd ever heard of him. That's one of the great mysteries of life as far as I'm concerned. The only other station we get is the low-power public-access station from East Millinocket. They have a video camera mounted up in one corner of the paper mill. It's aimed down at the floor so you get to see who's workin' what shift and so forth. If you don't come from that town, it's not all that interestin'. I'll usually switch channels after three or four hours.

Well, at any rate, on this particular afternoon, I was inside restockin' the shelves while Unc set out on the porch for his afternoon nap. There's a lot of work to stockin' shelves in them little stores. You've got to have a whole variety of items designed to appeal to all types of folks. But there's one thing I can't seem to get used to. You see it in every one of them country stores. You walk in the door and glance around and it's bound to catch your eye. Generally it's on the counter next to the cash register, a jar half full of this murky lookin' water, and floatin' in that water you'll see about a half dozen pickled eggs. How anyone could eat one of them nasty things is beyond me. Whenever I see a jar of pickled eggs it brings to mind all sorts of uncomfortable questions. Who ate the last one? In what year? What did they use to fish 'em out with? Those sort of questions are hard to ignore, I told Unc once.

"Unc," I says, "I believe, if I was starvin' to death on a desert island, and I crawled up over a sand dune and seen a jar of them pickled eggs, I'd turn right around and crawl in the other direction.'

"I know what you mean," says Unc. "I'd munch down a whole box of Slim Jims at one settin' fore I'd tackle even *one* of them nasty ol' pickled eggs."

Well, as I say, Unc was takin' his afternoon nap out on the porch. He was settin' in his rocker in the afternoon sun, and right next to him was this mongrel dog name of Queenie that hangs around the store lookin' for handouts in the summer. There they were the two of 'em sleepin' like babies, when this big car pulled up out front. Biggest car I ever saw. It was half again as long as a good-sized dory, with them fake wire wheels shinin' in the sun and all. I couldn't get a look at the license plates, but it was obviously from someplace out west. Most likely Massachusetts.

When the driver rolled his window down I got a pretty good look at him. A mighty impressive fella too. Fancy jacket, silk tie, big diamond rings on every finger. At first glance I thought he might be an Amway salesman. Then he yells out the window at Unc. "Hey, old timer," he yells.

Unc opened one eye, and you could see even at this early stage he wasn't enjoyin' the conversation.

"Ayuh," says Unc.

"I just thought I'd check with you before I got out of the car. Can you tell me, does your dog bite?"

Unc took a long look at the fella. Then he took another long look at old Queenie sleepin' on the porch next to his rocker.

"Nope," he says, "my dog don't bite."

Encouraged by this, the gentleman opened his car door and headed for the front steps. He'd barely hit that first step when old Queenie jumped up, barkin' and growlin', and tore into the fellow with a vengeance. He high-tailed it back to his car with the dog muckled firmly onto his leg. He shook her loose and jumped inside. Then he just sat there glarin' at Unc from the driver's seat. You could tell he was quite put out. Finally he lowered the window just a crack and yelled up at Unc, "I thought you said your dog don't bite!" "Well," says Unc, "mine don't. But ol' Queenie there sure does."

As that fella drove off in a cloud of dust, I'm sure he felt as though he had been unfairly taken advantage of and maybe even singled out for abuse. But the truth is he just happened to be the latest in a long stream of passersby who had run afoul of Unc's wit. Another example happened back in the hippie days of the sixties.

I remember it was fairly late one evenin' and this hippie van pulled up out front. It was an awful lookin' thing, bright orange with peace signs and flowers and stuff spray-painted from one end of it to the other. Two hippies with long hair, love beads, earrings, sandals, and so forth climbed out and came into the store. They poked around a bit and then asked Unc if he had any Grateful Dead tapes. Unc said he'd check, but the closest thing he could find was *Ernest Tubb's Greatest Hits,* which didn't seem to interest 'em too much. They poked around a few more minutes and finally the tall one says to Unc, "I don't suppose you've got any live entertainment in this town?" "Well," says Unc, "looks like we do now."

By this time you're apt to be gettin' the impression that Unc is a real hard-hearted type of individual, but nothin' could be further from the truth. As a matter of fact, he's probably one of the most generous public-spirited folks you'll ever run across. There's even been a few times when his generosity got him into trouble.

In the old days Unc took great pride in decoratin' the store for the Christmas season. He'd plan all year long how he was gonna improve his display. One August afternoon he was flippin' through a gift catalog when he stumbled upon the perfect centerpiece for the coming Christmas time. It was advertised as a "semi-life-size genuine styrofoam sculpture of Santa and his eight reindeer," complete with mountin' hardware and lightin' for a dramatic rooftop display. Well, once Unc saw that, he just had to order one for the roof of the store.

He sent right away, and even though the ad said to "allow six to eight months for delivery after your check clears," it arrived just a few weeks later. It was so impressive that Unc had all he could do to keep from puttin' it up that day (September 25th), but he decided to hold off at least until after Halloween.

November 1st dawned clear and cold, and Unc was up on the roof of the store bright and early installin' his display. By about four in the afternoon it was all in place, and everyone agreed it was the fanciest thing they'd seen around here in years. When sundown came, Unc flipped on the roof-mounted floodlights and the effect was real breathtakin'. In a matter of hours folks from all over stopped out in front of the store gazin' up at that marvelous display.

In the next few days it got real chilly, and we had at least an inch or two of new snow each day. Even though Thanksgiving was still three weeks off, it seemed the whole town was gettin' into the Christmas spirit. Entire families would load into their pickups and drive down to the store at dusk. They'd just set there drinkin' Moxie and eatin' cheese nips as the snowflakes drifted down around 'em. When the sun went down, Unc would step out onto the porch, wave at the crowd, and flip the switch that lit them floodlights. The crowd would cheer and honk their horns. It was quite a spectacle.

Then one night disaster struck. It was a Friday night near closin' time, and we were inside cleanin' up when we heard a big car pull up out front. The doors opened up and several men got out. They were hollerin' an carryin' on in such a way that we just naturally assumed it was a carload of them out-of-state hunters. They drive all the way to Maine lookin' for deer, but they usually find a good deal more beer than deer.

Next thing you know they quieted right down. Then we heard some noise like they was rummagin' around in the trunk lookin' for somethin'. And then all Hell seemed to break loose. Gunshots started blasting every which way. Unc and I dove under the counter, knockin' over a whole rack of girlie air fresheners right on top of us. We lay there scared to death until the gunshots stopped, and by and by we heard that car's engine start and the whole crew of 'em just drove off down the road. We lay there another minute or so until we were pretty sure they wouldn't be back.

Slowly we got up and went out front to see what the damage was. From the tracks in the snow you could fairly well piece together what had happened. Looked like there were about eight of them hunters in that car. Apparently when they got out and looked up, they mistook them styrofoam deer for the real thing, and started blastin' away at 'em with everythin' they had. Now, as I've said before, Unc is a pretty reasonable man and truthfully it didn't bother him so much that those fellas shot up his display like that. But what really got him upset was that once they'd blasted the deer to pieces, they proceeded to climb up on the roof, drag 'em down, strap 'em onto the fenders of their car, and head on down the road with 'em.

I tried my best to console him. "Look at it this way, Unc." I said. "Somewhere down in New Jersey there's bound to be a freezer load of styrofoam marked 'deer meat.' "

Unc just grinned, comforted by the thought that he'd still get the last laugh after all.

Our Boy Hubert

Our Boy Hubert

I don't know as I've ever introduced you to our boy Hubert. It's a little bit hard to really describe Hubert. For one thing, he lives in the barn out behind the trailer. He sleeps in a 1958 DeSoto that he reconverted into a bedroom. One thing I'll say for Hubert, though, is that he's real good with his hands. He's numb as a hake, but he *is* good with his hands. You heard of folks who don't know nothin'? Well, Hubert don't even suspect nothin'.

You'll always find Hubert tinkerin' around on some mysterious project or other. Like this last summer he was hard at work rebuildin' the engine of our old Dodge pickup so it would run on sawdust and hen dressin', which are real abundant natural resources out our way. It was a hot afternoon, and I was inside takin' a nap on the couch when I heard this explosion that sounded like a nuclear bomb going off out by the barn. I dashed out the door and ran around back expectin' somethin' horrible. When I got out there all there was left of

that old pickup truck was the four wheels and the bare carcass. I glanced around without seein' hide nor hair of poor Hubert. Just then I heard a rustlin' noise up above my head, and glancin' up, I saw Hubert caught about thirty feet up in the branches of the old maple tree. He was covered with soot, but he appeared to be all in one piece, and I noticed that he was still holdin' the steering wheel from the pickup. "Have a bad accident, son?" I queried. "No, thanks," he hollered back, "I just had one."

Mother and I do worry sometimes about Hubert. He's real clever with them inventions of his, but he can't seem to make any money with 'em. We figured it was just a matter of time before the right project came along, and sure enough one day it did.

Once a year Mother and I take a trip down to Portland, to do our Christmas shoppin' and just see the sights. On our last visit to the city we noticed a whole bunch of these video game parlors. It seemed as though there was one on every street corner. Out of curiosity we poked into one of 'em. It was dark as a closet shelf in there. All the games were lit up with pictures of rocket ships and dragons and Lord knows what all else. But the thing that struck me the most was the amount of cash them kids were pourin' into them machines.

After we left I couldn't help but think that somebody could make a lot of money by designin' one of them games specially for Maine kids. Instead of all these crazy space things, it could have somethin' runnin' around the screen that our local Maine kids could relate to.

It was just the project for Hubert. We explained the idea to him, and he set to workin' on it the next mornin'. For the better part of two weeks you could hear Hubert thrashin', clankin', and mutterin' to himself out there in the barn, pretty near around the clock. Finally he came in one afternoon and told us the thing was finished. We hurried right out behind

him, and as soon as we stepped inside the barn I could see Hubert had done a wicked fine job on this one.

The outside of Hubert's video game wasn't all cluttered up with these weird paintings. The whole thing was just nice weathered barnboard (of course, bein' a little damp that day, it smelled a bit like hen dressin'). The screen was from an old Philco TV, and all the buttons and stuff were right out of that '58 DeSoto. I noticed as I looked it over carefully that there were two separate slots where you could put your money in. When I asked Hubert about this, he was real proud of himself. Bein' aware of the tourist business, he had designed the game so it would take Canadian money. "Yup," says Hubert, "she'll take that Canadian money all right. She just won't give you a whole game."

Then the big moment came. I stood in front of the screen and dropped my quarter in the slot. The screen lit right up, and you could see a kind of maze of twisty roads with little digital spruce trees sprinkled around the edge of 'em. Next thing I know, down from the top of the screen comes this little digital pulp truck. Looked pretty realistic too. It had half the wheels off the ground on the right corners, and every now and then a digital log would drop off the back.

I was busy watchin' them pulp trucks wind down through the roads while Hubert explained the rest of the game. When you think you've got the timin' on them trucks, like how fast they're goin', which road they take, and so forth, you push one of the buttons on either side of the machine and along the bottom of the screen runs a little digital skunk. Now, the object is to hit as many of them skunks as possible with your pulp truck before the time runs out.

It was a great idea and I was some impressed with Hubert's work. I was sure we had the ticket to fame and fortune right in our own backyard, that is, until I actually hit one of them skunks with my pulp truck. I was curious that there wasn't any noise at the point of impact. I mentioned to Hubert that part of the fun with these games is hearin' them bells go off to let you know you've scored a hit.

"I got somethin' different for that," said Hubert, just as my nostrils filled with the unmistakable odor of fresh skunk. "Ain't that somethin', Daddy," said Hubert enthusiastically. "Don't you think that's wicked realistic?"

For a minute I couldn't say anythin'. We just stood there breathin' them fumes. Finally I turned to Hubert and put my arm around his shoulder. "Son," I says, "you done real good. You're a good boy. Particularly good with your hands. You're numb as a hake, but you *are* awful good with your hands."

Hubert Trains His Dog

When Hubert was growin' up, he always loved to play with other kids. Trouble was, other kids got tired of playin' with Hubert quite a bit sooner than he got tired of playin' with them.

Hubert always did have peculiar ideas about how things oughtta be done, which was apparent even back then when he kept comin' up with new rules for all the games kids have been playin' for years. 'Course the other kids didn't see nothin' wrong with the original rules, and that led to all kinds of problems.

For instance, when the boys organized a baseball game, they'd set it up along traditional lines. They'd have a pitcher, a batter, two teams, outfielders, and so forth just like old Abner Doubleday designed it. The pitcher would throw the ball, the batter would swat at it, and the runners'd go around the bases in the reg'lar order. Nobody had any complaints about the system. Except Hubert.

When it come Hubie's turn to pitch, he figured it'd be harder for the batter to hit the ball if the pitcher rolled it like a bowlin' ball. Hubie was right, of course, in his own weird way. Fact is, it was downright impossible to hit the thing unless the batter swung at it like he had a golf club. Hubert just figured that added excitement to the game.

The result of Hubert's tinkerin' with rules was that anytime he was involved in a game, the whole thing would grind to a halt and everybody would end up bickerin' and not havin' any fun at all. So it wunt too long before the other kids realized that any game they was plannin' would go a whole lot smoother if Hubert was somewhere else. He ended up spendin' more and more time by himself. Mother and I got worried about the boy bein' alone so much, and we decided maybe the best thing would be to get him a pet.

One Saturday mornin' we all piled into the pickup and headed down to the Pittsfield animal shelter to get Hubert a dog.

Everybody knows there's somethin' special about the relationship between a boy and his dog. But when the boy in question is our boy Hubert, the dog had better be somethin' pretty out of the ordinary if we expected it to take on the assignment.

When we got to the shelter there was all kinds of animals barkin', squawkin', and meowin' to beat the band, and the smell in that place would've embarrassed a skunk. We told the lady at the front desk we was lookin' to adopt a pet, and she ushered us in with the assurance they was all up for grabs.

Now nobody likes to mention the fact, but we all know what happens to them little puppies and kitties after they been at the shelter a couple of weeks. Hubert seemed to absorb this concept right off, and he made a beeline for the last row of pens where the most desperate cases waited just around the corner from you-know-where.

The minute I laid eyes on that pooch I knew we was in for an adventure. If there could ever be a canine version of Hubert, this critter was it. The dog was a mixture of several large breeds and a couple of small ones, which brought up uncomfortable images of the considerable gyrations that must of took place in order to bring that beast into existence.

It was love at first sight. That dog looked at Hubie like he'd found his long-lost pal, and Hubie returned the favor. I mean it. The very same look came across both their faces at the same moment. You might think it would be hard for a dog and a boy to get the same look on their faces at the same time, but I swear it's the truth.

As Mother and I signed the papers, Hubert lugged the puppy out to the truck. I've never seen two livin' creatures as happy as them two was at that moment. Hubie had finally found the ideal playmate. The pair of 'em was livin', breathin' proof of the old adage "Ignorance is bliss."

First thing Hubert had to do was come up with a name for the pup. He finally settled on Snowball on account of the color of the dog's fur, which was black, brown, and white. I didn't even bother trying to figure that one out. As long as Snowball didn't object, it was OK by me.

After settlin' on a name, Hubert started trainin' Snowball to do a few tricks. It was obvious right away that Snowball shared Hubert's unique way of interpretin' instructions. Hubert would pick up a stick, heave it off into the puckerbrush, and yell "Fetch!" Snowball would go boundin' off in hot pursuit, thrash around in the bushes, and emerge at a gallop, tail waggin' and ears flappin', and deposit the prize in front of Hubert.

Only trouble was, whatever Snowball brought back bore no resemblance to the stick Hubert tossed out. Old hubcaps, antique medicine bottles, a generator from a 1949 Hudson

Hornet, you name it, Snowball would find it and deposit it lovingly at his master's feet. Was Hubert upset? Not hardly. He understood the rules of the game as well as the dog did. With a pat on the head and a word of encouragement, Hubert would toss out another stick. No doubt about it, they was a perfect match.

Things went along pretty well for a couple of months. Then Hubert run across an ad in the back of an old *Mechanix Illustrated* magazine. That advertisement changed our lives forever. It was situated right smack-dab between "Can You Really Buy Surplus U.S. Army Jeeps for $44?" and "Finish Life at Home in Your Spare Time!" The ad had a picture of a German shepherd lookin' right atcha with a forlorn expression and a caption that read "Teach Your Dog to Talk!" It went on to say that for $19.95 they'd send you an audiocassette and phrase book guaranteed to teach any dog to talk in thirty days or your money back. Whoever wrote that ad must've had Hubert in mind.

Hubie turned in all his bottles, borrowed a couple dollars from Mother, filled out the mail-order coupon, and sent off for Snowball's correspondence course. About two weeks later it arrived by parcel post.

In the weeks that followed we hardly got a glimpse of Hubie and Snowball. For hours at a stretch they just stayed in the barn practicin' their lessons. Mother and I knew what was goin' on, but frankly we figured that as long as they was happy there was no harm done. That just goes to show how wrong you can be.

Almost a month to the day after that mail-order course arrived, Mother was havin' a few ladies from the church auxiliary over for afternoon tea. They was just takin' up the subject of food baskets for the starvin' kids in India when Hubert and Snowball burst into the den.

"Mama!" cried Hubert. "It worked! I taught him to talk, I really did!"

The ladies exchanged knowin' glances. They were all aware of Hubert's hare-brained projects, and their sympathy for Mother was evident.

"That's nice, dear," Mother said as casually as possible.

"No, I mean it," Hubie went on. "He can really talk. Wanna hear him?"

It was clear there was no way out. "Why I'm sure we'd all be delighted, wouldn't we ladies?" Mother said with a note of urgency.

" 'Course, of course," the ladies indulgently replied.

The followin' demonstration took everybody by surprise. The church ladies was operatin' on the assumption that if Hubert had managed to teach his dog to talk, it would be along the traditional lines. Stuff like "What's that thing on top of the barn?" "Roof, roof." Or "How does sandpaper feel when you touch it?" "Ruff, ruff."

What they got instead was a lengthy monologue from Snowball on such absorbin' topics as effective methods of avoidin' flea bites, how to approach a postman when he's not lookin', and a truly movin' soliloquy on the grace and charm of the next-door neighbor's poodle, who happened to be in heat that month.

All in all, I'd have to say things worked out for the best. Mother's church group eventually got over the shock of the encounter, and Hubert learned a valuable lesson. Even if you succeed in teachin' yer dog to talk, you'll eventually have to face the fact that a dog just ain't got much to say!

Hubert Doesn't Get Religion

Mother and I have always been the first to admit that our boy Hubert is a numb kid. But, once you accept the obvious drawbacks, there's a lot of good points about numb kids. For one thing, there is nothin' on the face of this earth more enthusiastic than a numb kid. If you have a numb kid (or even if you *are* a numb kid) you'll know what I'm talkin' about. It don't matter how many times Hubert tries somethin' and falls flat on his face, he's ready to get up and try it again five minutes later. As far as I can tell, nothin' this world dishes out can do much to dim the enthusiasm of a numb kid.

I remember when Hubie was just a boy, maybe eleven or twelve years old. He was wild about fishin'. Every time me and the boys went on a fishin' trip Hubert wanted to go with us. Ayuh, Hubert wanted to go fishin' in the worst way (which was the way we knew he'd go if he ever did go). Of course the boys all knew how numb Hubert was and they didn't want

him taggin' along makin' a pest of himself. I can't say I'm proud of it, but from time to time we'd been known to play some pretty nasty tricks on Hubert to avoid havin' to bring him along.

I can recall this one time. It was a long Labor Day weekend as I remember. Me and the boys had planned a trip up to Moosehead Lake in Greenville. Naturally we were careful not to let our plans leak out to Hubert. We backed the pickup truck into the driveway. It had the camper on the back with all our gear stowed inside and the canoe lashed onto the roof. We left it idling in the driveway while we went inside to pack some food for the trip.

Just about then Hubert come home from school on his bicycle and instantly grasped the situation. He took one look at that rig idlin' out front and a wave crashed across the barren shores of his mind . . . FISHIN' TRIP! He didn't waste any time. He ran right to his room, grabbed his rod, reel, tackle box, and all the rest of his fishin' gear and ran out and stood right next to the driver's side door of the idlin' pickup. He was grinnin' from ear to ear. He figured as long as he was standin' there, there was no way we could go on that trip without him.

He was wrong. We took the car.

As I've said many times, numb as he is, Hubert has always been a good boy. Never got in any trouble all the way up through school. Not until just lately that is. And it was only that darned "numb kid" enthusiasm that got him in trouble this time.

Hubert was all excited about his science fair project last spring. I'll have to admit it was a pretty ingenious idea he come up with too. He decided to build a solar collector on the side of the barn outta used hubcaps. Now, I've seen plenty of folks start in on this type of project, but I don't recall anyone gettin' one finished, wired up, plugged in, and ready to go. I was pretty impressed. Of course he had dawdled a little bit along the way. So, as the deadline for the science fair approached he was still lackin' a couple of hubcaps and all his regular sources for that sort of stuff was pretty much tapped out. That's when Hubert's enthusiasm overrode his better judgment.

Hubert knew if he was gonna win the science fair he needed to get two more hubcaps and time was runnin' out. Hubert also knew that the sheriff's cruiser was generally parked at the Dunkin Donuts over to Newport, and that the car had the perfect size hubcaps to finish his solar collector. It was a bold plan all right, and Hubert mighta got away with it except that he failed to take into consideration as he was pryin' away with his tire iron, that the sheriff was still settin' in the cruiser.

Well, the law took his clean record and vacant brain cavity into consideration and decided that rather than givin' Hubert a ticket they'd let him off with just a warnin'. I had sincerely hoped that would be the end of it. But, in a small town things don't always work out that way. In the next edition of *The Valley Times* (or "The Valley Crimes" as it is locally known),

there was a full account of Hubert's extra-curricular science fair activities, right there in black-and-white in the "Town Tattler" column.

I s'pose if it had stopped there we coulda just moved on. But nothin' ever seems to be that simple where Hubert is concerned. As fate would have it there was a new preacher who had just moved into the area a few days ago. I mean this fella was brand new, fresh minted, just graduated from the Bangor Theological Cemetery and he was right "on fire" to fight evil wherever he might find it. Unfortunately he found it in the "Town Tattler" column of *The Valley Times!*

Now I oughta mention right here that this particular "man of the cloth" was not associated with any actual religion you ever heard of like the Protestants, or the Catholics, or any of them. Nope, this fella was hooked up with some little make-it-

up-as-you-go-along outfit whose worldwide headquarters and Bible school was located in a plywood cabin out on a back road in Palmyra. They did have a name painted on the outside. As I recall, it was something like THE BLIND FAITH BRETHREN OF THE POWERFUL PRESUMPTUOUS ASSUMPTION OF GOD'S WONDERFUL PLAN FOR YOU. I can't say I ever studied their theology too close. But, even a casual run-in with a batch of 'em on a street corner some Saturday morning will clue in the average citizen to the fact that these folks generate a lot more heat than light.

Be that as it may, as soon as the newspaper hit the stands, that new preacher was on the phone with me tryin' to set up a meeting with Hubert. The preacher was sure that Hubert's run-in with the sheriff was only the beginning of a long ride down the slippery slope to perdition. I tried to explain about Hubert bein' a good boy but numb-as-a-hake and so forth. But it was pretty obvious that this fella had worked up a good head of steam already. He was going to come over and try to set Hubie's number twelve sneakers on the path of righteousness with or without my say-so.

There wasn't a lot I could do. So, I invited him to come on over around three when Hubie would be home from school. I did try to give him some advance warnin' though. Just before he hung up the phone I said, "Pastor I don't mean any disrespect. I know you feel that it's your duty to come over and try to talk some sense into Hubert. I just want to warn you before you get here, greater ships than yours have run aground on these rocks!"

I'll say one thing for the fella. He was right on time. Just about two minutes before three he pulled up outside the trailer in a little "leopard car." I don't know if you have leopard cars where you live. But Maine is right chock full of 'em. A good example of a Maine leopard car would be somethin' along the lines of a Chevy Chevette, vintage around 1981, with bondo slapped into most of the major rust holes, sheet metal pop-riveted onto the tops of the fenders and a variegated paint scheme featuring small spots of spray primer equally distributed from the front bumper to where the rear bumper used to be. That's the leopard effect. (Sorta like a Maine version of a Jaguar.)

As he got out of the car I noticed that he was listin' about thirty-five degrees to starboard. By the time he come all the way around to my side I could see why. That preacher was luggin' one of the largest Bibles ever produced. It was bright blue leather with a big gold buckle on the front and it must have weighed the better part of seventy pounds. He musta noticed me gawkin' at it 'cause he hefted it up to eye level to give me a better look. "Mighty fine lookin' Bible you got there." I said sincerely.

"That it is!" he replied with obvious pride. "This one originally sold for $500 on the Jimmy and Tammy show on TV. I picked it up at a yard sale in Canaan for only $1.59 last summer." They say the Lord works in mysterious ways.

Well, I took him and his Bible out back and introduced him to Hubert. Then I went inside the trailer and peeked out the back window. I knew whatever happened next would be too good to miss. The preacher didn't waste any time on formalities. He just plunked that massive Bible down on the front wheel of an old John Deere tractor Hubie was tinkerin' on and he started in to preachin'. Well sir, you never heard preachin' like that fella done that afternoon. He started right off in Genesis, cranked her right up through the gears till he hit Revelations, and then without hardly pausin' to catch his breath, he slapped her into reverse and charged right back down through

the whole thing again. Hubert was treated to so much hellfire and brimstone preachin' that it come darned near meltin' the vinyl sidin' on the back of the trailer.

But there was a serious problem. Even though the preacher was givin' this his best shot, not one word of it hit Hubert! I mean to say not a single syllable penetrated that thick Hubertian skull. To put it another way; the lights was on, but nobody was home! And, the preacher was in a panic. He was just about out of ammunition and he hadn't come within a mile of hittin' the target. Desperate for some way to get his point across, he struck upon an analogy.

He had been tryin' to impress upon Hubie how we should never steal, 'cause stealin' is a form of greed, and greed is a sin, etc. To drive home the point he reached in his pocket and pulled out three coins. As he held up his outstretched palm to Hubert, Hubert looked down and saw three coins: a quarter, a dime, and a penny.

"Hubert!" roared the preacher, "what if I told you that if you took that quarter you would have to spend eternity in Hell?!" When the preacher hollered that word *Hell*, a look passed over Hubert's face. The preacher, of course was ecstatic! Assuming that he had finally gotten through to this poor befuddled sinner. Naturally, anyone who knew Hubie could have straightened him out on that point. You see, this look that come across Hubert's face had nothin' to do with the coins, the threat of eternal damnation, or anything else the preacher was sayin'. Nope, it was just a look that passed across Hubert's face every now and then. Sorta, like a cloud passin' across the face of the moon. In other words, it didn't mean a thing. But as I've said, this preacher was desperate so he took it as a sign that he was breakin' through. "On the other hand," he bellowed, "if you only took the dime, you'd only have to go as far as Purgatory!" Hubert figured that Purgatory was probably a lot like Hell with the thermostat turned down a few notches. The preacher wound up and delivered what he hoped would be the game winning pitch. "But, Hubert," he said gently, drawing the boy into his confidence, "if you only took the penny you could spend eternity in Heaven." He stood back and delivered his ultimatum. "Given that choice Hubert . . . what would you do?"

At that point Hubert sorta came to and realized that he'd been asked a question. He didn't recall everything the fella had said, but he thought he'd got the gist of it. He reached his hand out and snatched all three coins from the preacher's palm. Then, he looked up and grinned. "Now that I got all three coins," he said, "I figure I can go anywhere I want."

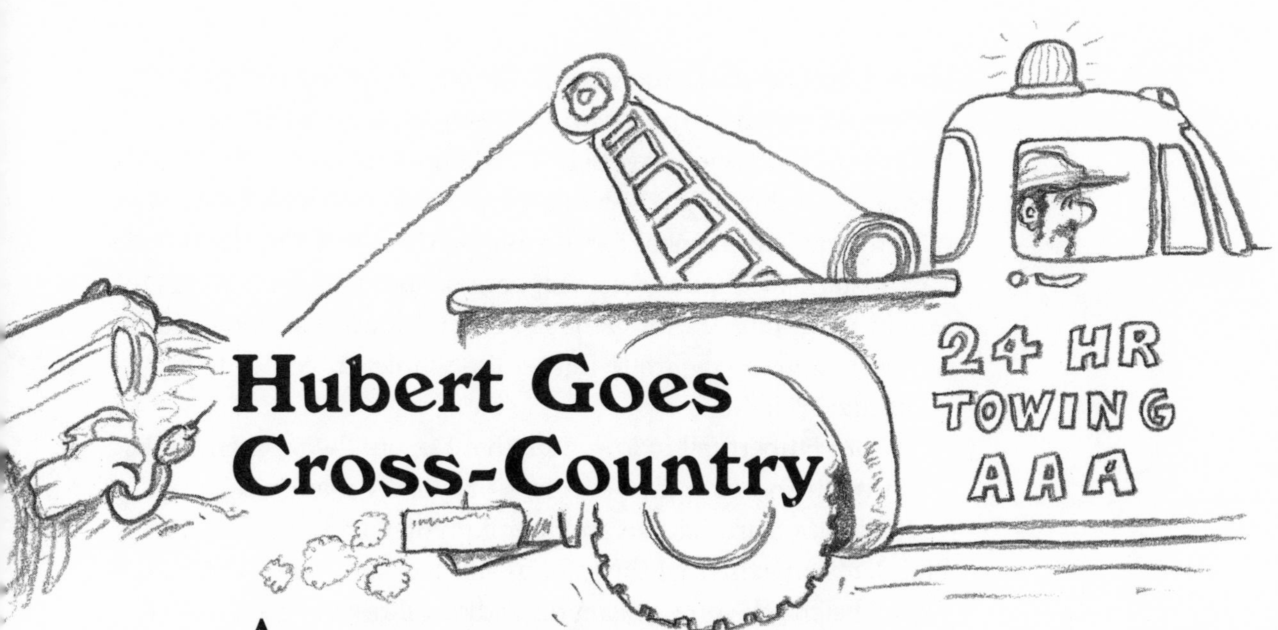

Hubert Goes Cross-Country

An often overlooked aspect of numb kids in general and our boy Hubert in particular, is that deep within the recesses of their minds there lies a certain warped form of genius. I realize that it's not an easy concept to swallow, but it's a fact. The Huberts of this world have an uncanny knack for what a well-educated person might refer to as "creative problem solving." For those of you who are still skeptical, here's a classic example of what I'm talkin' about.

I believe I've mentioned to you at some point in this narrative that Hubert's primary residence is in a beat-up 1958 DeSoto. If you haven't driven a '58 DeSoto lately, consider yourself lucky. I'm not insinuatin' that them old DeSotos aren't wicked sharp in the stylin' department. (Take a good long look at the tailfins on Hubie's car, and the Batmobile starts to look as boring as a checker cab.) It's when you start tryin' to keep 'em runnin' for more than five or ten minutes straight that serious problems crop up.

I first noticed how mechanically challenged Hubie's DeSoto was when I drove it off Honest Fred's used car lot over to Newport (just one week before Fred got indicted). I headed for home, and the ol' girl seemed to be chugging along fairly well. Then I made the mistake of turnin' on the radio. This impulsive act instantly cut our cruisin' speed by about 50 percent. It's a good thing Hubie don't smoke, 'cause I found out later that if you push in the cigarette lighter the whole car comes to a shudderin' halt.

But Hubert fell in love with that DeSoto the moment he laid eyes on it, and over the years he's practically made a religious ritual outta tearin' down and rebuildin' it. Given his skill level (zip), it's amazin' that the radio is still workin'. Come to think of it, I'll betcha the only reason the radio still runs is that Hubert ripped it out and stuck it in his snowmobile two winters back.

You might think that havin' nothin' but failure to show for all his hard work would be a mite depressin' for the young lad. But that just shows that you don't know nothin' 'bout Hubert. With all of his numb-kid enthusiasm intact, Hubert has never abandoned the notion of resurrectin' that car. To Hubert that old rusted hunk of Detroit iron is the ticket to fulfillin' one of his lifelong dreams: a cross-country motor trip. "See the U.S.A. by car!" he'll holler as another dead alternator flies off into the puckerbrush. Ayuh, he may be number than a pounded thumb, but Hubert has always had big dreams. And one night he found the means to make this particular dream a reality.

It was well after midnight. Me and mother had been asleep for hours and Hubert was slouched down on the sofa with his eyes glazed over, watchin' images flicker across the TV screen, when suddenly an advertisement come on that snapped him right to attention. It was an ad for the Triple A Motor Club. The pitchman was sayin' how great it was to be a member of this club. He talked about how they'll help you plan your trip and get you special discounts on stuff. And while this sounded just fine to Hubert, it wasn't special discounts or trip plans that set a match to the soaked-in-kerosene dishrag of his imagination. Continuing his sales pitch, the announcer promised the nation's insomniacs that once you join up with the Triple A Motor Club (operators are standing by) you'll get your own personalized plastic membership card. On the back of the card there's a toll-free phone number. Dialin' that number will connect you to your new pals at the Triple A. But—here's the part that really ignited Hubert's brain cells—when you call, those nice folks at the Triple A are obligated to send a tow truck out and tow you up to one hundred miles—in any direction—as often as you need it—anyplace in the United States of America—twenty-four hours a day! It was an offer he couldn't refuse. Hubert dialed the number. Ten minutes later and $39.95 poorer, he was a proud Triple A member.

The operator had been careful to mention to Hubert that it would be several days before his membership card arrived in the mail, and that his account would not be active until he called in and confirmed receipt of the card, etc. I'm sure the telemarketin' folks made her say all that stuff for technical reasons. But for all the effect it had on Hubert, she coulda been bayin' at the moon. Even though it was still pretty near the middle of the night, Hubie grabbed his flashlight, headed out behind the trailer, and began packin' up the car for his long-awaited cross-country journey.

Once he'd crammed everything he owned into the car, Hubert rounded up a few of his friends. (It was touching how many of 'em were willing to pitch in and help him get ready

to leave.) Working together, they managed to push the heavily laden ark of a car out into the front yard. Taking up his position behind the massive steering wheel, Hubie sat there, 'round the clock, eyes glued to the mailbox, anxiously awaiting the arrival of his Triple A membership card.

It arrived about three days later. In a matter of seconds Hubert was on the phone, card in hand, breathlessly giving directions to the tow truck driver. A half hour later the truck hove into view. With yellow lights flashing and warning beepers wailing, the truck backed into the yard. Lowering the towing hook from a crane in the back, it muckled onto the front bumper of the DeSoto, and with Hubert honking the horn and waving goodbye, disappeared down the road in a cloud of dust.

They towed him as far as Gardiner, unhooked the car and headed back to the garage. The truck was barely out of sight before Hubert was back on the phone with his new friends at Triple A requestin' another tow. Of course they had to oblige him. After all, he was a member. This time the truck dragged him almost to Kennebunk.

Now, you can laugh at Hubert all you want, but last week he sent us a postcard from Yellowstone National Park. I'd say the boy's doin' all right for $39.95!

Trailer Life
WELCOME
TO OUR PAD

Trailer Life

Everybody has their own ideas about where they'd like to live. Some like a big old farmhouse, or a little cottage by the sea, or even one of them geodesic domes. But I maintain that you've never really experienced life until you've lived in a trailer.

Now, I wouldn't have said that a few years back, but Mother's been hooked on 'em for years and she finally dragged me down to the Open House they had at St. Albans Mobile Homes over to Newport. I went mostly for the free coffee and doughnuts, but once I was there I began to get the fever.

They were havin' a special sale that week on "demos." (A demo is just like a regular trailer, except the salesman lives in it.) We took the tour, and he explained how everythin' in the trailer is coordinated right from the factory. In other words, your rugs and furniture and lamps and so forth all match up with each other, and that's important. If you stop and think about your own house or your best friend's house, you most likely realize that it's chock full of the most awful assortment of mismatched odds and ends you ever saw. Most of the furnishings in our place looked like they didn't belong in the same county with the other stuff, much less in the same room.

Well, when you buy a trailer, all that aggravation has been taken care of for you. Everything matches everything else, and it's top quality merchandise too. Even the artwork on the walls is all coordinated at the factory. And it ain't the cheap type of stuff you probably got hangin' on your walls, the type that's done on paper or canvas or somethin'. Nope, only the best in these trailers . . . genuine velvet! With your choice of all the classic themes, like Kenny Rogers sweatin', or conquistadores, or the one that Mother really loves—a matched set of them poor little kids, with eyes about the size of large dinner plates, standin' in an alleyway holdin' a little puppy or kitty. Real art!

Well, Mother and I purchased our trailer, and we were lucky enough to get us a little piece of land where we could make sure that the slab was built real close to the road. Personally I can't see the point of havin' your trailer set way back six or eight feet from the pavement. I'd say it ain't more than three feet from my door to the shoulder of Route Two, and the convenience is amazin'. For one thing, I hardly lifted a snow shovel last winter. Them big semis and log trucks come barrelin' by, and the wind from their passin' just blows the snow clean off the whole front lawn. And in the summertime, if I leave the windows open, them big rigs stir up such a breeze it's just like free air conditionin'.

But the real joy of trailer livin' don't come from the coordinated interior or even a prime location like we've got. The one thing that makes a man's trailer his castle is lawn ornaments.

Now, when we signed the papers on our place, we were fortunate enough to receive a year's free subscription to *Trailer Life* magazine, and the very first copy that arrived was the big annual summer lawn ornament edition.

We read that from cover to cover and learned that there's a real art to settin' up your lawn ornaments so's to get the maximum effect and enjoyment out of 'em. For one thing, you don't just go out and buy a raft of stuff and strew it around the lawn. First you have to pick a theme for your display. After thinkin' about it we decided we were gonna try "wildlife."

Our first purchase was a plastic duck and a set of little ducklings, which we positioned way down to the north end of the lawn headin' in a southerly direction. Then on the south end headed north we've got a gray styrofoam goose and these little goosies sort of aimed on a collision course with them ducks, but of course they ain't movin'. Just about dead center in between 'em we got one of them nice little cupolas. That's a rig that looks like a well house, only there's no water under it. It's made of cedar shakes, and it makes a dandy place for a half dozen of them styrofoam gray squirrels to perch.

Sprinkled around between the ducks and the geese we've got a bunch of other little creatures, like two cement donkeys with geraniums sproutin' out of their backs and a little ceramic frog on a lily pad holdin' a sign that says "Welcome to our Pad." And we've got quite a handful of them wooden willygig type ornaments that move when the wind blows. There's four mallard ducks with wings that rotate in the breeze, six pinwheel daisies, and a wooden hound dog that acts like he's chasin' a rabbit every time one of them semis drives by.

Mother had to go over to New Hampshire recently for a big Mary Kay convention, and on the way home she stopped and picked up some of these birds they got over there. They're a largish sort of bird, with pink color to 'em. They've got a long droopy neck and two real skinny legs made out of wire. I believe the proper name for 'em is a flamenco. Well, anyhow, she picked up about two dozen of them birds, and we've got 'em arranged in a row runnin' pretty near the length of the trailer. Looks real sharp.

Of course about every four feet or so down the length of the lawn we've got one of them exploded tires. Have you seen 'em? It's a marvelous use of technology. I don't know quite how they do it, but somehow they take a regular tire like you've got on your car and they explode it inside out so it looks kind of like a baked potato. The edges are sawed off into a jagged pattern like Jughead's hat in the comics. The deluxe model has the tips of them jagged edges painted in opposite colors. One will be dayglow orange and so forth right clear around the tire. That might not sound too complicated or artistic, but just try it yourself sometime. I'll guarantee you'll end up with two of the same color at the end.

Of course, we had to leave room somewhere to put our lawn chairs. We've got a matched set from the K-Mart, the kind you can stretch out and take a nap in, but the lawn bein' so narrow and all we had to set 'em up facin' each other end to end. Otherwise your feet would be stickin' halfways out into the roadway. We noticed that settin' in that position it was a little difficult to see the whole lawn, so we got one of them chrome balls that reflects a panoramic view of the whole spread. There's few experiences to match settin' in them chairs just gazin' at the reflection of them magnificent ornaments in that blue ball.

Now, there's one area that sometimes gets overlooked when folks are decoratin' the outside of the trailer. That's the space right around the front door. Of course, we've got a few of them round cement patio blocks runnin' from the steps to the road and right at the end there's a mailbox shaped like Uncle Sam with his hand stuck out. But the space I'm referrin' to is on the side of the trailer just to the right of the front door. We've got three of them little ceramic kittens crawlin' up the side of the trailer, and just to the right of 'em there's a name-plate that Mother ordered from one of them skinny little gift catalogs that comes in the mail around Christmas time. You know the kind I mean. They specialize in items that you've never heard of before, but once you see 'em you've just got to buy one. Like them little plungers that's designed to remove your blackheads? Now, you never thought of that, but seein' it in the catalog you won't rest till you've tried one out.

Well, she ordered this nameplate from the same catalog. It's made out of "wrought plastic" (just like wrought iron, only more durable), and it has an old-fashioned carriage dragged along by a team of horses. In white letters underneath the horses it just says "The Hendersens." That ain't our name. It was a "demo" model, and I can tell you there's times when that nameplate comes in mighty handy.

For instance, let's say you're settin' inside on a quiet Saturday afternoon havin' a few beers and watchin' big-time wrestlin' on TV. All of a sudden you hear the doorbell ring. Since you ain't expectin' anybody, you get a little put out by it. Slowly you get yourself up out of that lounge chair and open the door only to find a couple of Moonies or somebody else you don't know or care to. Well, the first thing they're apt to ask (havin' read that nameplate) is, "Is Mr. or Mrs. Hendersen at home today?" In which case you can simply say "no," shut the door, and go back to what you were doin'.

Say whatever you want. Live wherever you've a mind to. But as for Mother and I, for pure comfort, convenience, and graceful livin', we'll take our trailer any day of the week.

The Black Fly Festival

The Black Fly Festival

One reason Maine is such a popular spot for folks to visit in the summertime is the wonderful variety of fairs and festivals goin' on. I've been to a lot of 'em myself. I try to make it up to Eastport every year for the vacant building festival. And of course, Mother and I wouldn't miss the Wiscasset worm days. But for pure local Maine fun and good times you've got to head up to Rangeley in the spring, for the annual Black Fly Festival.

Rangeley is one of the prettiest towns in the state, and lots of folks go up in the winter for the skiin' at Saddleback Mountain. Matter of fact, years back I used to play music in the lounges up there, always hopin' I'd get hooked up with the ski crowd. You know the ski crowd? Them young good-lookin' folks from away, that drives Porsches and got money?

To tell the truth, I never did really hook up with the ski

crowd, but I ran head on into the skidder crowd, and that's a whole different crew altogether. And the skidder crowd is the one you're likely to see at the Black Fly Festival. It runs for a whole weekend with all types of events and contests, but everyone agrees that the highlight of all the activities happens on Saturday night at seven-thirty right in the center of town at the I.G.A. parkin' lot. The annual Miss Black Fly competition.

Don't get me wrong now, this Miss Black Fly competition ain't just another beauty contest. (As a matter of fact, beauty don't hardly even enter into it.) These girls are all from the skidder crowd, and they're all good strong hefty Maine girls. Last year's winner probably weighed in at about 235 pounds, and for the talent part of the competition she carved a life-size statue of Michael Jackson out of pulp wood with her chainsaw. They made a video tape of her doin' it. Only took her about an hour and it looked just like him.

In order to get a good position to see the show, Mother and I arrived down at the parkin' lot about six-thirty, and even then you could just feel the excitement. Crowds of people from all over the place was swarmin' in. Not to mention the black flies. The stage was a flatbed truck hung with buntin'. They had originally planned to buy a set of them big spotlights like you see at one of them gala Hollywood movie premieres. As I say, they wanted to get 'em, but I guess the town budget wouldn't stretch that far. But they did pretty good just the same. They parked the two police cruisers facing the stage and then backed 'em up so their hind wheels were down over the curb. Then the Girl Scout troop colored each headlight a different color with magic markers. When the deputies flipped them high beams on, the effect was real professional lookin'.

CAT
LIFETIME
NRA
MEMBER
GASOLINE

When seven-thirty rolled around, the three finalists walked onstage in their swimsuits and the crowd was cheerin' like mad. The MC announced through a bullhorn that this was serious business. Just like the Olympics, he said. The contestants had been instructed that they couldn't use any chemicals. No Off, or Ben's 100, or old-time woodsmen's fly dope. Then he stood back and the girls posed in their swimsuits. You could hear a pin drop as the whole crowd watched. Them black flies started swarmin' somethin' fierce. Finally the girl on the left broke down and swatted one of the critters and was automatically eliminated, leavin' only two standin' Them two battled it out for the better part of three minutes until the one on the right finally gave out and started swattin' them little demons left and right. The crowd let out a cheer as the MC placed the Miss Black Fly crown atop the winner, knowing' that she had passed a test of stamina, endurance, and character that few people could ever match.

The Wig

The Wig

Old Elva Tuttle lives up on the ridge in the farmhouse his family built over a century ago. He's always been a good neighbor, but ever since his wife passed on a few years back, he's had a tendency to keep to himself a good deal. They were real close, them two, married the better part of seventy years, and he took her passin' kind of hard.

I remember the day she died. I was down to Berry's Pharmacy in Pittsfield, havin' a cup of coffee and catchin' up on the local gossip. There were two elderly ladies settin' on the stools alongside of me, and one of 'em turns to the other and says, "Did you hear that Maybelle Tuttle passed away last evenin'?" "No," says the other one, " and furthermore I don't care a thing if she did."

Well, that struck me as kinda hardhearted, so I perked up a bit and began to listen close.

"You can't mean that!" says the first lady.

"I most certainly can," the other lady replied. "I never cared for Maybelle, and I don't care what anybody thinks of it."

"Well, at least," says the first one, "I expect you'll pay her the courtesy of attendin' the funeral."

"I will not!" came the reply. "If she ain't comin' to mine, I'm darn sure not goin' to hers."

You know, some folks are just like that, but even so I felt bad for old Elva. I knew he missed her somethin' fierce and he was just pinin' away for her month after month. So I took it upon myself to stop by once or twice a week and try to cheer him up.

One afternoon we were sippin' hard cider on his front porch and I suggested that he might try goin' out on a Saturday night to one of them dances they hold down to the Grange Hall in Palmyra village.

"You know, Elva," I ventured, "there's a number of very attractive widow ladies that goes to them shindigs. If you was to go a few times you might even meet somebody you'd like to settle down with."

I could tell right off that Elva was cool to the notion of going out socializin'. But I must say I couldn't really understand exactly why. Well, we kept talkin' as the sun went down, and several glasses of cider later I had my answer.

Once he got loosened up a bit, Elva admitted that he was a little self-conscious about his looks. He said that as he got on in years (he was eighty-seven at the time) he'd begun to notice that his hair was thinnin' out at a pretty alarmin' rate. He had his mind made up that even as lonely as he was, he couldn't take the embarrassment of askin' a lady to dance, with his old bald head hangin' out as it was. After hearin' the nature of his complaint, I knew I had a remedy.

I excused myself and went back to the trailer. I got hold of last week's copy of the *Grit* newspaper, where I remembered I'd seen this certain advertisement. I leafed through it, and sure enough there it was, a great big ad on the next to last page.

The ad was for a modern acrylic wig, one size fits all, made out of durable, weatherproof, fade resistant, acrylic fiber. It was guaranteed in writin' to make any man look twenty years younger, which would give Elva the youthful charm of a sixty-seven-year-old. Not only that, but it came complete with a tube of this new formula adhesive designed to give the wearer hours of security even in the most inclement weather. To prove this last point, they had an actual unretouched photo of a satisfied customer, hangin' about six feet off the ground, suspended by a backhoe hooked onto the wig. I must admit it was pretty impressive.

I sent in the twenty bucks and had 'em deliver the goods to Elva in a plain brown wrapper so as not to arouse suspicions down to the Post Office. It came a few weeks later and I could tell I'd done the right thing when I saw Elva the followin' Saturday mornin' at the hardware store. He had that wig on, and he was grinnin' like a dog eatin' bumblebees.

About six-thirty that evenin' Mother and I were settin' out on the front porch when she says, "I guess Elva's goin' to dance down to the Grange Hall tonight." I cocked my ear in the direction of Elva's place. "Ayuh," I says, "sounds that way to me."

That part about the listenin' probably needs a bit of explainin' for folks who ain't familiar with Elva's social habits. First of all, when he goes out for the evenin' Elva always takes his horse and buggy. He claims it gets him where he wants to go and, besides, hay is a good deal cheaper than gasoline. And for an important occasion, he always douses himself quite liberally with that Four Roses toilet water. Now, I don't know what the ladies think of that stuff, but I can tell you for a fact that the deer flies are crazy over it. They swarm so thick around him that you can hear this low hummin' noise comin' from up the road even before Elva makes the crest of the hill.

By and by he pulled up out front of our place lookin' as dapper as I've ever seen him. He had on his best Sunday-go-to-meetin' suit with a fancy broad-brimmed straw hat, and

you could see that wig pokin' out from under the edges of the hat. He was some old proud of that wig.

We chatted for a few minutes, and then he said he had to get goin' or he'd be late for his date. Before he left, though, I made him promise to stop by in the mornin' and let us know how the evenin' went. Off he trotted like a school kid goin' to his first social.

Next mornin' about nine o'clock Elva stopped by. I've never seen him look so downtrodden before or since. "Well," says I, "how'd everythin' go last evenin'?"

"Probably one of the worst nights I ever seen," he replied mournfully. "Oh, it started off all right. After I come by your place I headed out towards Route Two. Once I got onto the paved part and got up a little speed, I lost most of the deer flies. But when I got to the crest of the hill up there by the Palmyra Consolidated School, I slacked off the reins so's to enjoy the view. Y'know, it's a nice sight out across them cow meadows just as the sun is settin' on the hills. Well, anyways, I was sorta admirin' the view when a gust of wind come up real strong off Sebasticook Stream on my left-hand side. Next thing I knew that wind had caught the brim of my straw hat and lifted it clean off my head.

"I guess I ain't allowed enough time for the glue to set up on the new wig, 'cause when the hat blew off, it snagged onto that wig and flung it halfway out into the meadow. Now, luckily I was wearin' my trifocal glasses, but even so I have to admit they ain't got a settin' for searchin' through a cow pasture at sundown, but there was nothin' else to do but try and fetch that wig back, so I climbed down off the wagon and commenced to searchin' where I thought it might have landed. It wasn't such a pleasant pastime as I'd been lookin' forward to. But it could have been worse, I guess. After about thirty minutes of searchin' I finally found that wig, although I'll admit I tried on several before I got the right one."

Snappy Answers

Snappy Answers

I don't want to give you the impression that Unc has some kind of monopoly on one-liners. You've already been introduced to my neighbor, Blinky Pinkham, and it is my considered opinion that when it comes to formulatin' and deliverin' snappy answers, Blinky is an all time Hall-of-Fame candidate.

I have no idea just what the reason is, but if you'll take the time to look into it, I think you'll find that most of the really great practitioners of the art of snappy one-liners tend to be elderly folks with quite a few miles on the clock. Not all, I'll grant you, but most. It also helps if they occasionally take a nip of somethin' stronger than Haley's M.O.

Well, old Blinky was ninety-seven years old last time I checked and as sharp as a wedge of Vermont Cheddar. Havin' lived almost a century, Blinky's seen plenty of hard times,

which also seems to be an advantage when reachin' for a snappy answer.

Physically, Blinky has the look of a well-broke-in union suit that's been hung out to dry in a stiff March breeze at about 10 degrees Fahrenheit. In other words, he's still all in one piece but seeyin' him don't give ya a burnin' desire to find out how he accomplished that feat. Of course, like most of this breed, Blinky has a natural fondness for what he always refers to as "hootch." And he's never been shy about takin' a good long snort when the mood struck. You might even say that Blinky was the town drunk. Although, to be strictly accurate, I'd have to admit that Palmyra was so small, we never really had a town drunk. Everybody just sorta took turns.

One thing I will say for Blinky, though, is that he was never a fella who'd get behind the wheel and drive when he'd been drinkin'. He didn't drive much anyway but he was always stone sober when he did. Not that he wasn't prepared for the worst, you understand. Blinky always carried a spare bottle under the front seat of his truck (just in case he got stuck in a blizzard or at a three-day revival meetin'), and one day that bottle came in pretty handy.

Blinky was backin' his '53 Ford pickup truck out onto Route Two one mornin' at about eight o'clock. He was headed for the Gateway Diner in Newport to have his daily dose of coffee and conversation. Just as he was pullin' out, he heard a high-pitched whine like three or four lawnmowers runnin' full tilt on airplane fuel. A second later he saw a flash of bright red come flyin' up over the hill to the west. Then he heard an awful crunch as somethin' travelin' approximately the speed of sound smacked into the rear of his truck, slid underneath of it, and pushed the whole steaming mass of wreckage into the middle of Route Two.

Blinky jumped outta the cab and determined pretty quickly that he wasn't hurt. What turned out to be a bright red low-slung sports car had run right up under his back bumper and lifted the whole truck about two feet in the air. Blinky crawled underneath and dragged the driver of the sports car out of the smoldering wreck. Amazingly, he wasn't really hurt much either. A few cuts and scratches was about it, but he was pretty shook up just the same, and he was cryin' and moanin' and carryin' on somethin' wicked. Between gasps and sobs he explained to Blinky that the sports car was a brand new Ferrari (easily worth the price of six or seven good trailers). It got worse from there. The man said that the car actually belonged to his brother-in-law and that he'd just "borrowed it" for a little joy ride. It was pretty clear that this young fella was on the verge of a nervous breakdown.

Sizin' up the situation, Blinky walked back to the cab of his pickup and fished around under the seat until he struck upon his spare pint of Jack Daniels. As he walked back to the sobbing sports car driver standing next to his brother-in-law's

XXX

crumpled Ferrari, Blinky opened up the brown paper bag, uncapped the eighty-proof bourbon, and handed it to the young man.

"No thanks," he said, "I don't drink."

"Go ahead," said Blinky in a grandfatherly tone. "You're awful upset. It was only a car. Nawthin' to have a heart attack over. Besides this'll calm you down a mite."

"I guess you're right," he said, and with that he took the proffered bottle and drained off several long pulls. As the liquor began to hit him he let out a long sigh. "Well, old timer, I guess you're right," he said, voice slurring slightly. "What's done is done. We might as well relax a little."

With a lopsided grin he passed the bottle of whiskey back to Blinky. Blinky promptly recapped it and started back toward the cab of his truck.

"Hey!" shouted his newfound friend, "aren't you going to have a drink too?"

"Oh, I will in a while," said Blinky with a grin, "but I think I'll wait till after the police get here and write up the accident!"

Most of Blinky's snappy answers are dispensed down at the Palmyra General Store which sets right in the center of town and dispenses a lot of other important items too, like jumper cables, Slim Jims, and Moxie. (Only in Maine could someone invent a drink that tastes so unbelievably awful that you are compelled to buy another bottle, and another bottle, and another bottle just to convince yourself once more that, yes it really does taste that bad!)

Stores like Unc's and the Palmyra General Store are still a part of the landscape in Maine. Although often colorful and distinctive, these old stores can pose a serious hazard to the wayward traveler in need of advice or directions, while remaining painfully ignorant of the gauntlet he or she must run in order to obtain such information.

The chief obstacle presents itself in the form of a handful of locals, *a k a* "the regulars" who seem to be a permanent part of the furniture, maybe even the architecture of the place. They are mostly (but not always) older men like Blinky, frequently glowing with a rich patina of age and grime which is a near-perfect match for the oil-soaked, well-worn, uneven floorboards of the store. You'll find these fellas standing around the woodstove, kicked back in creaky wooden chairs, or leaning on ancient, dusty wood and glass display cases.

The unsuspectin' visitor, walkin' into the store for the first time, is apt to view this little crowd as simply a chance gathering of natives, laughin', smokin', and swappin' lies to pass the time of day. Nothin' could be further from the truth! This innocent lookin' group is, in reality, nothin' short of a SWAT team composed of past, present, and future grand masters of the fine art of the snappy answer. If you ever find yourself in this situation, my advice would be to pick up some cheese nips, a can of Moxie (you can discard the Moxie later), and possibly a road map if they've got one. Whatever else you do, don't even think of engaging one of "the regulars" in even the briefest of conversations. Let me put it this way: In the old "spider and fly" scenario—you ain't the spider here chummy!

Blinky heads up a typical gang of Maine geezers down at the Palmyra General Store and woe unto the passing stranger who seeks to engage any of 'em, especially Blinky, in a bit of idle chit-chat. I've been privileged to observe Blinky in action dozens of times. One of the most memorable happened two summers back.

It was a swelterin' hot day. The temperature was hoverin' around ninety and Blinky and "the regulars" were engaged in a heated debate which threatened to crank the in-store temperature up over three digits.

The topic was a common one for Mainers in the summer. It is generally summed up by the question, "How bad was it over to your place last winter?" Each geezer in turn attemptin' to top the last one in his description of waist-deep snow, fifty-below windchills, and so forth that *he* had experienced in his

DOWNEAST HUMOR
S.W.A.T.
TEAM

particular neck of the woods. You'd never know from eavesdropping that at least half these guys spent the winter in Florida.

The debate was steamin' along full tilt, when a car pulled up out front. While they continued to comment on the miseries of winter in Maine, the boys did not fail to note that the plates on the car were from Arkansas. With a little luck, the driver would be too. Sure enough, the weary traveler stepped into the store and paused a minute to take in the scene. Blinky and the boys were hard at it, gripin' and moanin' about week-long blizzards, black ice, everything up to, and includin', the lack of a January thaw.

Upon hearing the litany of weather-related complaints, the stranger felt compelled to jump into the conversation. It was a fatal error on his part. "I couldn't help overhearin'," he drawled, "all yer talk about the bad weather up here in Maine. Well I got news for you fellas. We've got somethin' down in Arkansas that's worse than any weather y'all ever seen around here."

"Is that so?" replied Blinky, deftly sinking the hook. "Now what might that be?"

"Well, old son," shot back the Arkansan with a hint of pride, "what we got down home is an Arkansas tornado. Ain't nothin' worse than an Arkansas tornado!"

"I'd have to disagree with you on that point," said Blinky. "I maintain that we've got somethin' here in Maine that's at least as bad as any tornado you folks have ever seen."

"What's that?" huffed the southerner.

"Well," said Blinky, "I'm talkin' about a Maine divorce!"

"No fair!" shouted the southerner. "I don't see any similarity between an Arkansas tornado and a Maine divorce."

"You probably don't," said Blinky with a grin. "But I can tell you from hard experience, if you get hit with either one you're gonna lose your trailer pretty darned fast!"

Naturally, Blinky and a lot of other Mainers wouldn't get the chance to crack half as many one-liners if it weren't for the overwhelming number of questions we get asked by confused tourists each year. You want to understand that central Maine in general, particularly the sparsely populated stretch of Route Two along which Palmyra is located, is not exactly the area that most people set out for when they plan to visit Vacationland. But, be that as it may, there are an awful lot of people drivin' around up here in the summer. I don't really know where they all come from, but I get the feeling that somebody, somewhere, told 'em all to get lost. And apparently they did. At least, an awful lot of 'em end up asking directions at the Palmyra General Store. Blinky is always ready to enlighten them.

On one particular day in early June, Blinky was settin' in the chair out on the front porch of the store (just settin' there

with one arm as long as the other, as he'd say). When he heard a car approachin' from the direction of Skowhegan. It was movin' right along and it sped through the center of town without so much as a tap on the brake pedal to acknowledge having been there. It wasn't too long though before Blinky heard the same car roaring back towards him from the other direction. Blinky had seen this sort of thing before and he sat forward in his chair anticipatin' the next few moves.

As expected, the car went sailin' through town just as fast as before. Only, this time it was headed in the opposite direction. Blinky noted that it was a blue Volvo 245DL wagon with Connecticut plates (you might have seen this one around, yourself). Blinky knew the drill. Every few minutes the car would come slammin' back and forth in front of the store. Sometimes a little faster, sometimes slowing as the driver glared around in frustrated confusion. Of course each time he passed the store the driver noticed Blinky noticin' him. It was, however, clearly a standoff. The driver was determined that he would not give up and ask directions. Blinky knew better.

Finally, the beleaguered Volvo pilot resorted to a last-ditch gambit occasionally used by out-of-state folks when they're totally lost ("turned around" is the Native phrase) on the back roads of Maine. He unfolded his road map and propped it up on the steering wheel in front of him as he buzzed past the store one last time. This is a very popular technique these days, kind of a do-it-yourself air bag, only a whole lot thinner.

The end of the exercise was as inevitable as Blinky knew it would be. The battered driver pulled his car onto the soft shoulder just opposite the store and sat there starin' at Blinky. Blinky stared back. The wisp of a smile floated across his face. The driver rolled down his window, his face red and puffy from anger and frustration. Bloodied but unbowed he waved the crumpled up road map out the window and screamed at Blinky, "How in the devil do you get to Bangor?"

"Well," Blinky mused contentedly, "most generally my brother-in-law takes me."

I suppose anyone is capable of comin' up with a snappy answer every now and then. But, I believe it takes a real Mainer to know which one is going to push you over the cliff and send you hurtling directly into the pounding surf on the rocks below.

Speaking of pounding surf and the rocky coast, reminds me that some of the most revered names in the pantheon of the snappy answer belong to the men and women who risk their lives each day tryin' to snatch a livin' from the briny deep. Growin' up in Boothbay Harbor I gained a deep respect for fishermen, lobstermen in particular.

One of the great lobstermen in our town (and there are many) is named Douglas Carter. "Dougie," as he is known to his friends (you'd be well advised to start off with somethin' more like "Mr. Carter, sir"), is a classic dyed-in-the-wool Maine lobsterman. Big, tall, and handsome; tough as nails, but not a bully. Whether he was haulin' ass in a souped up lobsterboat durin' the annual lobsterboat races, or haulin' traps in a snow squall off Outer Heron Island, Dougie Carter always had a knack for bein' where the action was. He was a natural born leader with a wild streak two lanes wide. Dougie just didn't seem capable of doin' anything halfway, which generally makes for a pretty dramatic life. I figured he'd either end up as a state police trooper or behind bars in Thomaston State Prison.

Apparently neither of those lifestyles appealed to him. Instead he became one of the founders of the Boothbay Region Lobstermen's Co-op. That's a place over on the east side of the harbor where once the lobstermen catch the lobsters, they bring 'em in, cook 'em up, slap 'em out on the wharf on a bunch of picnic tables and set back and watch the fun as thousands of tourists attempt to extract a meal from the vault-like hard-shelled crustaceans using tiny plastic knives and forks. It's darned good live summer entertainment for the locals—profitable too.

Due to the steady stream of tourists providing an equally steady supply of numb questions, most folks who work at the co-op can dole out a snappy answer with relative ease. As in so many others, Dougie Carter excels in this department.

He told me that on one particular summer afternoon he had come in from fishin', weighed his catch and was standin' up on the wharf havin' a cup of coffee. As he sipped the steamin' java from a styrofoam cup, he watched the brightly colored crowd of tourists milling around on the dock. The parkin' lot was almost full. It was going to be another good day of fishin' for tourist dollars.

Then he noticed a great long car slide into the parking lot and straddle the last two remaining spaces. Dougie could tell right off, without even glimpsing the plates, that the car belonged to somebody "from away." It looked like it might be a foreign make. Dougie couldn't quite read the flowing script on the deck lid. It looked like it mighta said "Cad Dillik." At any rate the darned thing was almost two Dodge Darts long.

The driver stepped out of the front door, turned to lock it, then headed down toward the crowded wharf. There was no question that this guy was a tourist. He had the outfit down to a T. He had the plaid blazer, the "salmon" colored pants, white shoes, white belt, silk shirt unbuttoned down to the navel with about sixty pounds of gold chains draped across the openin'. He was wearin' so many chains that you'd swear he just clipped out the front page of the latest Service Merchandise flier and glued 'er right on his chest. Dougie had him pegged right off. "That right there is an Amway salesman!" he stated with the certainty of a trained observer. Don't misunderstand my meaning here. Folks in Maine have always liked their Amway meetings. I'm not sayin' you're guaranteed to rake in a pile of money, but you can have a wicked good time at the meetings. That's worth quite a lot in itself on a long cold winter night.

Dougie noticed another thing about the fella. The man was walkin' straight in his direction starin' at Doug with a sort of mesmerized expression which the locals refer to as "souvenir lust." Plainly stated, souvenir lust is the overwhelming compulsion on the part of tourists to muckle on to something—almost anything—from Maine, shell out huge amounts of tourist dollars, strap it onto their car and drive home with it. Needless to say it's an affliction which we locals heartily encourage. If you know someone with a particularly bad case, send 'em up to Boothbay Harbor next summer. The folks at the co-op will make sure they're well taken care of.

When he got to where Douglas was standing, the tourist's eyes dropped to the weathered deck of the wharf. There, just alongside of Doug's right foot was a brand-new, never-been-fished lobster trap. I'm not referrin' to the newfangled wire-box style of traps either. This was a traditional Maine hardwood trap with hand-knit pot heads, and wooden lathes with leather hinges on the doors. Maybe you haven't seen one of these old fashioned traps for yourself. If you're tryin' to get a mental picture, I can help you out. They look exactly like a coffee table from L.L. Bean.

From the moment he caught sight of it the tourist was smitten. His souvenir lust meter buried its needle in the red, and he asked Douglas if by any chance the trap might be for sale. Dougie gave him the traditional Maine answer. "Ayuh," he said, "when it comes right down to it most things around here are for sale at the right price."

"How much will you take for that one?" stammered the excited tourist.

"Well," Doug drawled, "I 'magine I could part with that one for fifty dollars cash money."

"Oh gee," replied the tourist, "I really couldn't afford that much. Maybe I could look around down on the dock for somethin' I could get a little cheaper."

"Suit yerself," said Dougie. And, the tourist wandered off in search of another, more affordable souvenir.

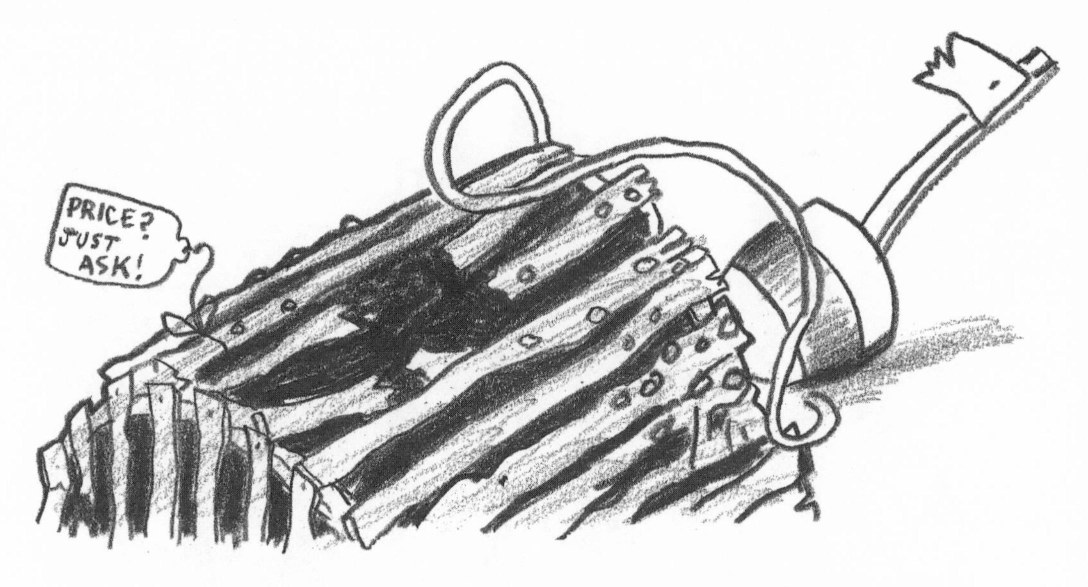

It wasn't long before his spirits brightened. There on the dock he stumbled upon a whole pile of lobster traps. They were just the ticket: old, weather-beaten, with dried seaweed hangin' off of 'em and the occasional sun-bleached fish head lurking in a far corner. Dependin' on your point of view, these traps were either scuzzy or "rustic." You can guess which interpretation this fella favored. With a spring in his step he ran up the ramp to find Doug. Of course, Dougie hadn't moved an inch. As the breathless tourist described the treasure he'd located, Doug interrupted. "Hold on there," he muttered, "I know the traps you're talkin' about and I can cut you a deal for one too. The only thing is, I'd have to get a hundred dollars each for them traps."

The man was flabbergasted. He just stood there sputterin' for a few seconds and then he dove in. "I don't understand how you can ask twice as much for those old broken-down traps as you do for that brand new one!"

"Oh," Dougie smiled, "that's not so hard to figure out. You see, them old beat up traps down on the dock, they belong to me. I don't have any idea who this new trap up here belongs to!"

As well known as he is as a world-class snappy answer man, Blinky Pinkham has other skills which enabled him to thrive on a dirt road in rural Maine. High on the list are a sharp eye for a bargain, and an almost genetic inability to let anything go to waste. The following incident will give you an idea of what happened when he brought both of those talents to bear at the same time.

When I lived in Palmyra, Blinky lived right next door to me, next trailer over, about five miles down the road. You could always tell his place because right out by his driveway he had an oak tree with a limb that hung out over his front yard. Hangin' off the limb was a 225-cubic-inch slant-6 Dodge engine block. Now, if you're not from Maine, that might seem odd. But folks out our way knew that Blinky hung that old engine block up there for a very specific reason. He'd expected to get a free valve job done on it.

It seems that, while he was pickin' up his mail at the Pittsfield Post Office, Blinky heard a rumor that the Whipple boys from over to Newport was goin' to automobile mechanic's school. The way Blinky heard it, they was desperate for some homework projects to practice on. Sensing a bargain, he put in a call right away. Unfortunately (like a lotta stuff you overhear at the post office), Blinky had picked up the general drift of the idea but he was kinda fuzzy on the details.

By the time the Whipple boys arrived at Blinky's trailer, the facts had begun to sort themselves out. The truth was that outta the nine available Whipple boys, only *one* of 'em was actually takin' any sort of mechanics course. That turned out to be a forty-eight-week correspondence course off the back of a matchbook cover. The part about needin' somethin' to practice on (and therefore workin' for free) was accurate enough, however, so Blinky decided he'd let 'em take a stab at fixin' his engine.

With the rest of the Whipple boys lookin' on, the mail-order mechanic began flailing away with a vengeance. Unfortunately his level of training hadn't proceeded much beyond reading the matchbook cover and daydreamin' about the profits. Although short on training, his enthusiasm for the task was boundless. Soon valve covers, spark plugs, and a bewildering array of assorted nuts and bolts filled the air in Blinky's front yard like a swarm of mechanized black flies.

Young Whipple was working fast and furious. Unfortunately there was trouble brewing just around the bend. After tearing the thing apart for about half an hour he ran head-on into the actual valves. It's pretty obvious that anybody plannin' to do a valve job ought to know at least somethin' about valves. It was also obvious that this fella didn't. He was beginnin' to look a mite sheepish when luck, in the form of a thundershower, stepped in and bailed him out. A clap of thunder exploded overhead, and rain started comin' down in buckets. The Whipple boys abandoned the engine block project and joined Blinky as he made a beeline for the trailer.

That rain storm just kept poundin' down on the roof of Blinky's trailer for days. While they waited for a break in the weather, Blinky broke open a few cases of his secret stash of Carling Black Label beer. By the time they came out of the trailer (about a week later) that engine block was still danglin' from the tree limb. Only now, it was hopelessly encrusted with rust. As Blinky recalled later, "She was just plain froze up solid as a block of maple."

But after starin' out his window for the past several days watchin' that engine block sway in the breeze, he'd sorta got used to the way it looked. A creative spark ignited in Blinky's brain. He rummaged around in the trunk of his car and dug out one of the three items that any good Mainer has on hand at all times: WD-40, duct tape, and bungie cords. Mainers know

that if you can't fix it with one of them three items, you might as well put it in the yard sale. Or you can always throw a blue tarp over it. That's good for a half dozen years, easy.

Blinky took his can of WD-40 and soaked the engine block from one end to the other and commenced to pry the rusted pistons out of the block. Presently they popped out as slick as a smelt swimmin' through a school of eels. After wipin' the whole engine block down and lettin' it dry out, he got a can of lipstick-red paint and slathered it on nice and thick. Once the paint was dry, Blinky proceeded to letter his name on the side in big white block letters.

So in the end Blinky wound up keeping all nine of the Whipple boys out of serious trouble for several days in a row, while simultaneously recycling a useless engine block into a sharp looking high-capacity mailbox that even the most snow-blind plow driver wasn't apt to smash into. Not too shabby for an old codger on a rainy week.

The Mary Kay Girl

The Mary Kay Girl

One of my favorite neighbors is Marlene, the Mary Kay girl. If you've never heard tell of that Mary Kay stuff, you've missed quite a lot. What it is, you see, is a whole raft of fancy cosmetics that women sell door-to-door to their former friends and so forth. One of the best parts of doin' Mary Kay is that after a woman sells a couple of tons of them cosmetics, the company gives her a free car. That's hard to believe, I know, but it's the God's honest truth. I've seen it with my own eyes.

Now some of the fellas around here ain't too keen on that Mary Kay. Matter of fact, there's a few of 'em that's dead set against it on the grounds it keeps their womenfolk out rammin' the roads at ungodly hours, sometimes as late as 7:30 or 8:00 at night. Personally, though, I have to say I've got nothin' whatsoever against them cosmetics. Matter of fact, they've made quite a few ladies out our way considerably easier to look at.

Marlene, of course, is a real charmer in her own right. Personality plus, that's what she is. And wicked cunnin', too. Even before she took up sellin' that Mary Kay, I had her pegged as a real fine specimen of feminine pulchritude.

First off, Marlene's got one thing goin' for her that most Maine men find darn near irresistible. She's a real good heavyset girl. I can't for the life of me see the attraction in them skinny girls you see on the covers of the glossy magazines at the checkout counter down to the supermarket. You know the type I'm referrin' to. They slouch around with a pout on their face like their dog just got run over. They're skinny as a rail fence, with their cheeks all caved in. And likely as not, they're only half dressed. Godfrey mighty! A girl built like that wouldn't make it halfway through a Maine winter. Sure, a fella might be tempted to gawk at them girls when he's buyin' this week's Megabucks ticket. But when it comes to warmth and comfort durin' a three-day blizzard, nothin' can compare with sheer physical bulk. Without strainin' the truth, I'd say Marlene'd dress out at 275 pounds or better.

About a year after she started sellin' them cosmetics, Marlene pulled up in front of our trailer in a great big pink Buick. She'd earned her free car. It weren't exactly spankin' new, but it was mighty slick lookin' all the same. Power everything on that baby. That front seat was as big and squishy as any sofa I ever set on. It had a power ashtray that'd practically jump onto your lap at the flip of a switch and even a power antenna. 'Course the antenna just had a bent coat hanger stuck in the socket, but it went up and down just the same. Marlene had the Whipple boys over to Newport chop off the body just behind the driver's seat and had a plywood flatbed built onto the hind end.

Say what you want, but one thing's for sure, you can haul a wicked load of cosmetics around on that rig. You go ahead and laugh all you want, but when Marlene pulls into the gravel pit on a Saturday night in that rig, she's *somebody.* The only complaint she's ever had about that car is that it came off the lot with one of them FM stereo radios, and she was a little peeved at havin' to order an AM converter in order to pick up the good stations.

Ayuh, I'd say Marlene definitely has a sense of style that's pretty hard to ignore. You take that little pooch of hers. Most folks out our way'll settle for a mess of beagles tied up out back or a couple of mutts lounging on the tailgate of the pickup. But not Marlene, no sirree Bob. She's got her some real class. When she got that job sellin' Mary Kay she hightailed it all the way up to Bangor and got her one of them fancy French "puddle" dogs. She claims they originally come from all the way over to France. Don't look a bit like a puddle in my book, but it does bear a pretty strong resemblance to a piece of fancy-cut shrubbery strainin' out at the end of that leash.

Now I got to admit I owe Marlene a personal debt. A couple of months back she invited Mother to one of them Mary Kay parties. You got to understand that them parties are one of the main ways them Mary Kay girls pump up the local clientele. They invite the ladies over for a free demonstration of their fine line of cosmetics, and when the party's over they send 'em on home with a free starter-kit of some hot-sellin' items. This is to sorta prime the pump for future sales. The idea is to get the new girls so fired up about the free samples that they'll join right up and start pushin' the stuff on their own.

Well, it just happens that on the very evenin' Marlene invited Mother out to that party, I'd made plans to spend the night out myself. It was league bowlin' night at Elsie's Candlepin Lanes down next to the laundromat. But come to find out Dewey Langley, best man on the team, had turned his ankle somethin' wicked tryin' to drop-kick a raccoon that had gotton into his trash can, and we ended up with a forfeit.

So that's how I happened to be home early when Mother got in from that Mary Kay party. She come a-bargin' through the door all in a tizzy on accounta missin' the first few minutes of Lawrence Welch, plopped them cosmetics on the kitchen table, and made a beeline for the sofa. She was so all fired wound up about that TV show she never even noticed me settin' there at ten past eight in the evenin', on league bowlin' night!

Once Mother was settled in the livin' room, I took a gander at the package she'd flopped down on the kitchen table. Darned if it wunt one of them free sample packs of Mary Kay stuff. There was powders, perfumes, nail polish, and just all manner of refurbishin' hardware designed to enhance the feminine mystique.

One item in particular just seemed to catch my eye. It was a pretty good size tube of lipstick, and (you can believe this or not, but it's true) it was the *exact same* color as that safety orange the deer hunters wear. I'm not kiddin'. You know what color I'm talkin' about. That special orange stuff that jumps out atcha. You see it all the time durin' huntin' season. Or in the off-season it's the same color the road crews and them flagpersons use while they're tyin' up Route One all summer long. Well, I'll be darned if it wunt the same color stickin' outta that lipstick tube.

Now say what you want about folks sellin' cosmetics door-to-door, but soon as I saw that lipstick my mind was set. All I can tell y' is I knew right then and there I'd feel safer ridin' in the car at night with Mother if she was wearin' that lipstick.

I figure it this way. What if we happen to be drivin' along a dirt road late at night and we get a flat or run out of gas or somethin'? Why, all Mother'll have to do is step out onto the shoulder and pucker up a few times at reg'lar intervals, and we'll have a cop there in no time.

The Teeth

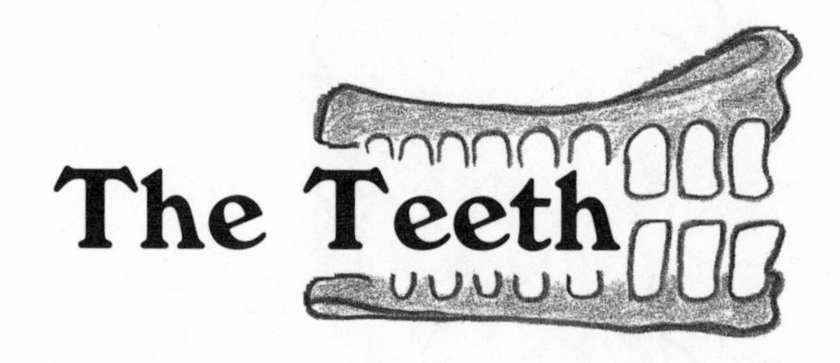

The Teeth

One of the luxuries of livin' in Maine is that you can still find a pretty decent selection of diners up here. In case you ain't been payin' attention, it's my sad duty to inform you that the good ol' owner-operated, fryolator-scented, greasy spoon American diner is without a doubt on the Endangered Species list. Diners are a vanishin' breed all over the country these days, but here in the Pine Tree State, I'm happy to report there's still quite a few of 'em open for business.

I don't mean to imply them fast-food joints ain't made some significant inroads. They're here, all right. All you got to do is cruise up Route One, and you'll find plenty of places loadin' folks up with an exact replica of what they're dishin' out from Timbuktu to Kalamazoo, along with enough paper goods and styrofoam to start your own bonfire.

'Course it's more'n just the food they serve that makes diners special. It's the whole feel of the places. Each and every

diner in Maine is an orig'nal enterprise. Lots of 'em have been run by the same family for generations, which is more'n you can say for them plastic burger palaces. You don't believe me? Next time you stroll through the golden arches, ask to speak with Mr. McDonald. He don't even exist! And although Roy Rogers is a real live person, you're not apt to find him hangin' out at one of his restaurants either. See what I mean?

On the other hand, if you was to stop by Moody's Diner some afternoon and ask to have a word with Percy Moody, you'd see right off that you was in a whole different ballpark. I ain't promisin' he'd give you an audience, but if you caught him in the right mood he might. The whole point is, there's just a different way of doin' things at a diner. If you've never tried it, you don't know what you're missin'.

At a diner things are different from the minute you walk in the door. First off, diners specialize in that homey lived-in look. Instead of hard plastic seats and bare, antiseptic walls that remind you of the waitin' room at the vet's, you're more likely to find a row of booths with soft, padded seats decked out with swatches of duct tape where the rips are. The counter is usually yellow or pastel green linoleum with cigarette burns on the top, old bubble gum underneath, and a worn, scalloped edge where a couple of generations of truck drivers have rested their elbows.

In a good diner, the owner is prob'ly somewhere out back. You can see the cook and the dishwasher through the skinny little window they pass the food through. The waitresses tend to be plump and friendly with names like Shirley and Elsa. And a diner is one of the few places left on earth where you can still find a professional waitress. I'm not talkin' about high school and college kids lookin' for part-time work or retirees supplementin' their social security. I'm talkin' about honest-to-goodness, been-here-35-years, veteran hash slingers. Walk into a really good diner, plunk yerself down, and ask the waitress what they've got for dessert. Without so much as pausin' for a gulp of air, she'll rattle off fifteen or twenty items, all the way from chocolate cream pie to homemade tapioca puddin'. Right then and there you'll know you're dealin' with a pro.

One of our favorite diners ain't really a diner at all. It's a truck stop, but it's got all the ingredients of a great restaurant in the finest diner tradition. To start with, it's been there forever, the kinda place where folks bring their grandkids to set at the same booth they used to set at when they was young. The place I'm referrin' to is just south of Bangor, right off Route 95. You can tell when you're close because the big rigs swarm around the place like hornets on an over-ripe peach.

When you pull into the parkin' lot you'll notice somethin' different right away. Stretched out in long rows are about thirty-five or forty gas pumps. Just downwind of the pumps is the restaurant. To make sure you don't miss the convenience of all them pumps, they have a tall sign that says "Dysart's Truck Stop. Eat here, get gas!"

Since most of the regular customers at Dysart's are truck drivers, the place is designed to make 'em comfortable. Some folks might get nervous eatin' a chicken-salad sandwich next to an almost life-size paintin' of an eighteen-wheel Kenworth Diesel headed straight at 'em, but it makes them truckers feel right to home. Over to the gift shop area are the necessities of long-haul truckin'. There's a good supply of tapes by such legendary artists as Boxcar Willy, Slim Whitman, and Utah Phillips, and Dysart's is one of the few outlets nationwide where you can still get the original version of Dusty Rhodes's country classic "If Ya Wanna Keep the Six-Pack Cold, Put It Next to My Ex-Wife's Heart" on eight-track cassette.

One Wednesday evenin' Mother and I decided to stop in to Dysart's around suppertime for some of their famous homemade chicken potpie. We were just settlin' into our booth when we noticed an elderly couple takin' their seats across the way from us. They both musta been ninety if they was a day, but from all the grinnin' and holdin' hands and so forth you'da thought they was a couple of school kids out on their first date.

He hung up her coat and helped her into her seat. Then he took out a little candle, lit it, and planted it in the truck-tire ashtray between 'em. We couldn't help glancin' at em. As I watched, I thought I remembered Paul Harvey sayin' on the radio that afternoon that a couple from Bangor, Maine, had won the Tournament of Roses. That's Mr. Harvey's way of

honorin' the couple that's been married the longest of anybody in the whole country. I leaned over and mentioned it to Mother, and she agreed they was prob'ly the very couple we'd heard about. Now generally we wouldn't be so nosy, but with such big celebrities settin' right next to us, we paid mighty close attention to what was goin' on.

They ordered a large bottle of Moxie and two glasses. After the waitress brought 'em, the man offered a toast. "I told ya so," I whispered across the table to Mother. "It's got to be them!" When the waitress returned, the man ordered two "Big Rigs," one for each of 'em. The Big Rig is Dysart's top-of-the-line entree, a great gigantic hunk of flame-broiled steak smothered in mushrooms and onions. I wouldn't order one unless you're real hungry.

Them two lovebirds went on cooin', holding hands, and gazin' into each others eyes right up 'til the meal arrived. That's when Mother and I noticed a curious thing. As soon as their dinner was laid out on the table, that old lady attacked it like a pit bull terrier. Knife and fork flyin', she dove into that beef like she was starvin' to death. Strangely enough, though, while she was flailin' away, her husband just set there grinnin' at her. I mean to say he never so much as picked up his fork.

The whole scene looked pretty odd. We didn't mean to stare, but they really did make quite a spectacle. After a few minutes, the waitress finally caught on and walked over to their booth. We couldn't help overhearin' the conversation.

"Well now," the waitress said. "How's everything goin' over here?"

"Oh, just fine," the man replied. "Couldn't be better."

"I just wondered," the waitress shot back, "if there was anything wrong with yer meal. I noticed yer wife here seems to be enjoyin' hers, but you haven't touched a bite all evenin'. What seems to be the problem?"

Suddenly the old gentleman begun to look pale as a ghost. He didn't say anything, but in a few seconds his color changed again. This time he was blushin' like a beet. The waitress saw he was embarrassed and jumped in to bail him out.

"I didn't mean to upset y', sir," she said. "I just wanted to make sure the meal was done to yer likin'."

Regainin' his composure, the old man turned to the waitress, gave her a little wink, cupped his hands, and whispered, "No, no, dear, nothin' wrong with the food at all. I'm just waitin' for Mother to get through with the teeth."

Teddy Roosevelt
Visits Greenville

Teddy Roosevelt Visits Greenville

Nobody would ever accuse Greenville, Maine, of bein' a bustling center of cultural activity. But over the years this little village has attracted a mighty impressive list of national politicians, business tycoons, and well-known sports and entertainment celebrities. What brings 'em to Greenville? Good question.

The founding fathers of Greenville plunked their town right smack dab on the shores of Moosehead Lake and just around the corner from Squaw Mountain. Whether it was the hand of divine providence, dumb luck, or more likely a little of each that drew the original settlers, it turned out to be a darned good move. You see, it didn't take long for word to get out that if you were lookin' for the best huntin' and fishin' in the state of Maine, you need look no further than Greenville. Moosehead Lake seemed to overflow with record-breaking togue and salmon, and the surrounding woodlands were chock-full of bear, moose, deer, and other game animals large and small. Yes sir, Greenville was a genuine sportsman's paradise.

By the turn of the century Greenville was geared up in fine shape to handle the surge of city-slicker "sports." Huntin' camps, sportin' goods stores, and local guides were almost as thick as the black flies. One of them stores was run by Nathan "Gramp" Shaw, a fixture in the town and well known to locals and sports alike. For the better part of ninety years he'd been offerin' unsolicited advice and commentary from behind the old brass cash register at Shaw's General Store.

Gramp Shaw had what folks back in them days referred to as a "contrary nature." If a particular point of view was held by the majority of Greenville residents, that was reason enough for Gramp to take the opposite tack. Most everybody

complained about his thickheaded positions on everything from the best black-fly repellent to local politics and world commerce, but few if any of 'em would argue the fact that Gramp's ideas added a dollop of spice to the constantly bubblin' conversational stew around the store's potbelly stove on long winter afternoons.

Now true to form, at a time when rural Maine was made up almost entirely of dyed-in-the-wool Republicans, Gramp Shaw was about the only registered Democrat in Piscataquis County. Nobody who knew him could possibly have expected otherwise. The year was 1904 and the ol' Rough Rider himself, Teddy Roosevelt, was runnin' for president, second time around on the Republican ticket. Folks in Greenville was foursquare behind old T.R. Not only was he a solid Republican, he was a well-known hunter, fisherman, and all-round sportsman to boot. Since Teddy had set up camp in the White House it seemed like all kinds of folks across America had caught the huntin', fishin', and campin' fever. As a result, a whole lot of shoe salesmen and postal clerks from places like Paramus, New Jersey, found their way to the camps around Greenville to follow the lead of the chief executive. No doubt about it, Teddy Roosevelt was darned good for the local economy.

So you can imagine the excitement that swept the village when they found out the president himself was comin' to visit. Word was that Teddy was takin' a weekend off from the pressures of the campaign trail to do some fishin' on Moosehead Lake.

The whole thing come about kinda sudden, but the town responded with unbridled enthusiasm just the same. By the time the presidential Pullman arrived at Greenville station early the following Friday, there was a sizable contingent of local dignitaries on hand to welcome the president and his entourage. The train depot was decked out with red, white, and blue bunting, and the remnants of the Twentieth Maine Regiment blew a passable rendition of "Hail to the Chief" as the president's car pulled to a shuddering halt at the platform. "Pug" Pinkham, head of the local grange, delivered a welcomin' address along with a key to the village and an invitation to speak at the grange hall that Sunday evening.

Gramp Shaw had enough gumption to miss the festivities at the depot, but even he couldn't resist the temptation to attend the grange hall meeting. Come Sunday night the old barnlike structure was packed to the rafters a good two hours in advance of the president's appearance. It was a warm August night, and the black flies and mosquitoes were jockeyin' for prime position. Kids swung their legs from the rafters overhead as pudgy ladies fanned themselves in the wooden folding chairs.

When the president arrived not a soul was disappointed. Teddy Roosevelt strode onto the stage at the stroke of 8:00 with a brand of self-confidence rarely glimpsed in that sleepy village. Ladies swooned and men applauded with gusto. From the first sentence it was obvious that the citizens of Greenville were enthralled.

All but one citizen, that is. As the masses cheered, Gramp Shaw slumped deeper and deeper into his folding chair and glowered and snorted at the speaker, obviously not impressed by his oratory.

Midway through the second hour of his talk, President Roosevelt fully appreciated the mood of his audience. He was preachin' to the faithful, so t' speak, and he knew he could do

no wrong. Flushed with his success, he committed a fatal error.

"How many of you out in this crowd tonight are registered Republicans?" he roared. The response was overwhelming. Every hand in that jam-packed hall rocketed skyward. Every hand, that is, but one. Gramp Shaw sat in the back row with his hands tucked neatly underneath his armpits and fixed the podium with a withering stare.

Now a lot of public speakers would have taken the crest of the wave and kept on goin', but this Roosevelt fella was one to take on a challenge. He noticed right away that there was only one dissenter in the crowd, and then and there he decided to tackle him.

"My good man," the president began, "would you mind standing up for a moment?" He said this in a tone that drew chuckles from the audience, virtually all of whom were aware of Gramp's political persuasion.

"Don't mind if I do!" countered Gramp, leaping defiantly to his feet to face the great man.

Roosevelt continued, "Would you mind explaining to me how it is that in an area so heavily Republican as this, you happen to be the only Democrat?"

"Well," replied Gramp, "that's pretty easy to figure. My daddy was a good Democrat, and his daddy before him. So likewise I'm a good Democrat."

"Well," says Roosevelt, not missin' a beat, "I suppose if your father and grandfather had been jackasses, you'd be a jackass, too!" The audience howled with laughter 'til the rafters rang with the echo of it. It had taken the president of the United States to do the job, but somebody had finally taken the wind out of Gramp Shaw's sails.

But Gramp wasn't quite finished. He kept up his steely-eyed glare, then a grin began to form at the corners of his mouth. His reply came slowly, accompanied by a twinkle in his old gray eyes. "No, sir, Mr. President," he replied. "In that case I guess I woulda been a Republican."

The Junk of Marshall Dodge

Marshall Dodge has for many years been acknowledged as one of America's premier native humorists. As a student at Yale University in the 1950s, Marshall and fellow Yale student Robert Bryan teamed up to produce a record album entitled *Bert and I and Other Stories from Down East*. In addition to being a bestseller, this record has stood the test of time to become the benchmark of Maine dialectal humor.

In the years following the release of the first *Bert and I* record, Marshall continued to collect and record the native humor of New England.

I met Marshall Dodge in the mid 1970s, and in 1980 we began performing together in the improvisational comedy team of Sample and Dodge. During the time we spent working together, I came to know Marshall as an inveterate collector of American folk humor. His apartment on Clifford Street in Portland, Maine, was constantly cluttered with a huge collection of antique books, records, and vaudeville posters covering virtually every aspect of our native humor.

A particularly engaging aspect of Marshall's personality was his penchant for distributing these items to whomever he thought could make the best use of them.

While in the process of working on our first comedy album, I received word that Marshall had been killed in a tragic hit-and-run automobile accident while vacationing in Hawaii. In the weeks that followed I decided to try to communicate my feelings about Marshall and his contribution to the tradition of Maine humor. I eventually came up with the following poem written in the style of one of Marshall's favorite poets, turn-of-the-century Maine humorist Holman Day.

The Junk of Marshall Dodge

I'd like to take your treasures,
And your trinkets, and your junk,
And load 'em on a boxcar in nineteen steamer trunks,
And get some played-out Engineer with steam still in his veins
From a life of haulin' folks and freight
From Boston up to Maine.

And I'd stoke him with the vision
And I'd enlist him in my scheme to run that train around the
world
Distributin' a dream.
And should he chance to ask me who might want this old hodge
podge,
I'd say, "This ain't just any junk, my friend,
It's the junk of Marshall Dodge."

With every detail overlooked, and only grace to guide us,
We'd steam across the continent with Marshall's junk beside us.
We'd run that train to every little town along the track
And stop and draw a crowd with whistles, bells, and union jacks.

And as they started gatherin',
Men, kids, and ladies large
I'd shout into my megaphone,
"Step up folks, there's no charge.
Feel free to touch the merchandise, it's more than rummage off
some barge.
This ain't any junk, my friends, it's the junk of Marshall
Dodge."

With the help of my assistants
(Just recruited from the crowd)
I'd push a button on the floor
And bring the music up real loud.
Bolts would snap and locks would slide. Them trunks would
open wide.
And men would peer, and ladies crane, to see what lay inside.

"Don't just stand there, folks," I'd tell 'em,
"Help yerself, this stuff is free!
With one small stipulation, now listen carefully.
You're free to take whatever strikes your fancy from this heap,
But only if you understand, it isn't yours to keep.

"It's only yours to spread around
and share with friend (and foe).
Now, if you can keep that promise,
Take somethin' before you go,
Like a book to send a relative
Who's homely as a stump,
Or a bicycle that's built for two
To help you o'er the humps.

"Or a tape machine to capture tales
Yer Uncle Jasper tells,
Or a boat that's called *The Bluebird Two*
To skim across the swells,
Or an anecdote to crack a smile
Across the sourest face,
Or a pin to prick the pompous
And put 'em in their place.

"It's all there for the takin', folks.
Pick well or not at all,
For there's many hamlets yet to hit while circlin' this ball.
And lots of folks along the way
In cities small and large,
Who just like you will gawk and peek
and smile
When we tell 'em (There's no charge!)
'Cause this ain't just any junk, we're handing out,
It's the junk of Marshall Dodge."

Set 'er Again

Set 'er Again

Bert and I was haddock fishin' this one particular summer. As I recall, the fishin' itself wunt all that good, but the weather was warm and sunny, which made fishin' a lot more appealin' than wadin' through a swarm of summer folks in town. So all in all we was havin' a pretty nice summer.

Along about the first of August, however, I noticed Bert actin' mighty peculiar. For more than a week he'd been arrivin' at the dock at the crack of dawn, happy as a clam in the mud and just burstin' at the seams with enthusiasm to go fishin'.

Anybody who knew Bert could tell right off that that kind of behavior at that hour in the mornin' just wunt like him. Not that he was bad tempered or anything. Just sort of a slow starter. Normally the first hour or so in the mornin' he just drug himself around, mumblin' and bumpin' into stuff. By the time we'd loaded the bait and the gear aboard and I'd poured a half dozen cups of black coffee into him he'd be talkin' in whole sentences. And by the time we got out to where we was gonna be fishin', he was passable good company.

But as I say, along about the first of August I seen a whole new side of Bert. When I pulled up at the dock he'd be there already loadin' the gear and whistlin' a tune chipper as a jaybird. After a few more days of this I couldn't stand it any more, and I begun to question Bert. After a little backin' and fillin' he finally admitted that the reason he was so happy to spend all his time fishin' was that his mother-in-law was visitin'. That cleared up the mystery in short order.

Now don't get me wrong. I've got nothin' against mothers-in-law as a general category. I'm sure there's plenty of great ones out there, and I'm a firm believer in the old adage "Behind every successful man there's a surprised mother-in-law." But the fact remains that I've met Bert's mother-in-law on several occasions, and I wouldn't wish her on my worst enemy, let alone my best friend.

To start with, this woman has got to be one of the largest creatures that ever walked God's green earth. She ain't just large, she's positively massive. Now I'd be the first to admit a preference for large women. I've always said a heavyset girl is shade in the summer and warmth in the winter. But that mother-in-law of Bert's has carried a good thing too far. Plus, in addition to her overpowerin' physical bulk, she's got a capacity for verbalization that would put them fast-talkin' TV evangelists to shame. That woman could talk the varnish off a canoe paddle before she really warmed to the conversation. Needless to say, I sympathized with Bert's dilemma.

On the last day of her visit, Bert was in rare form. I'da never thought a man could whistle, hum, and grin all at the same time, but I swear he was doin' just that when I arrived at the dock about 5:30 in the mornin'. "Great day fer fishin',

ain't it?" he bellowed as he tossed the bait barrel aboard. "I dunno," I muttered, "ain't been up long enough to notice." By this time Bert's jubilant spirit had started to wear on me a mite.

I cranked the engine a couple of turns, and she fired up and settled into her familiar coughin' and a-chuggin'. Bert cast off the bow line and the stern line, and he was just about to loose the springer line when I heard an ungodly wail outta him. Sounded for all the world like a cow stuck in a barbed-wire fence. I glanced up in the direction he was lookin', and I seen it, too. It was an awesome sight.

Sure enough, it was her. No mistakin' it. A great huge Cadillac with Massachusetts plates was barrelin' down the dirt road headin' straight for the dock. There was a cloud of dust spewin' out behind, and all the shock absorbers on the driver's side was shot to hell. She screeched to a halt just short of the dock, and through the dust cloud I could make out that great beefy arm of hers wavin' frantically out the window. Then I heard her bellowin' through the settlin' gravel. She was bound and determined she was goin' fishin' with us.

We knew right off we was trapped, and there wunt nothin' we could do about it. Bert heaved a sigh and made the lines fast. We headed up the ramp and made our way to the driver's door. Bert opened the door and we pried her out; then he got on one end of her and I got on the other, and somehow we maneuvered her down the ramp to the float. 'Course all this time she was talkin' a blue streak. Anybody with enough sense to leave the scene already had. Even the seagulls had high-tailed it outta there.

Somehow we loaded her aboard, centered her as best we could, and made our way out of the harbor towards open water. It was a nice mornin' weatherwise. The inner harbor was glassy calm with just a bit of sea smoke risin' off the surface. If anything, the tranquility of the scene spurred her on to greater levels of oratory, and she drowned out the engine without half tryin'.

But a funny thing happened as we approached the mouth of the bay. We begun to strike just a mite of heavy water. Nothin' serious, you understand, just a reg'lar five- or six-foot rollin' swell. As soon as we hit them swells, I noticed a change in our passenger. Her monologue definitely dropped several notches in volume. Bein' an old deepwater man, I took this as a sign, and sure enough, she begun to look a little green around the gills, and it wunt more than five minutes later she was up over the gunnels with an awful load o' chum. I could tell right then and there it was gonna be a long day.

By the time we'd anchored and started in to fishin', Bert's mother-in-law was feelin' mighty poorly. We laid her down in the bilge in order to make her more comfortable, and she settled into a reg'lar pattern of more or less sloshin' and moanin'. As the swells rocked the boat from side to side, she'd slosh almost up to the port gunnel. Then as the wave passed beneath our keel, she'd drift back to starboard and let out this low moanin' sound kinda like a barn door creakin' on a damp mornin'.

Back and forth she went, a-sloshin' and a-moanin' at reg'lar intervals. To tell the truth, compared to the yackin' she'd put up earlier in the voyage, that sound was almost soothin'. It was almost like that music they play down t' the K-Mart, just kinda background stuff that's real easy to ignore.

Meanwhile, Bert and I was havin' the best fishin' we'd had in quite a spell. On account of bein' so preoccupied with the fishin', I can't honestly say exactly what happened next. But apparently this wave come along that was just a little bit bigger than the rest of 'em. 'Course that's not unusual when you're a few miles out to sea. Well, I guess that wave musta smuck us a good whack along the starboard beam just as Bert's mother-in-law was on the upslosh to port. The only thing I can say for sure is that all to once she went sailin' over the side like the *Spruce Goose,* smacked the water with a thunderin' wallop, and proceeded straight to the bottom, slick as a cup o' custard.

I was surprised! I'da thought someone with that girth woulda had a certain amount of built-in flotation. No sir! Down she went just like a stone, and it was obvious the minute it happened that there wunt a darn thing we could do about it. So we kept on fishin'.

Towards the end of the afternoon we hauled in the gear and headed for port. We made the mouth of the harbor just about twilight, stowed the gear in the boathouse, brung the boat out to the mooring, rowed the tender back to the dock, and then Bert, of course, run right off to call his wife and break the news. 'Course she was mighty upset about the whole thing—anybody would be!—but we explained there wunt nothin' we coulda done about it.

As you might imagine, the next few days was pretty hectic over to Bert's place. The family arrived from all over. Then realizin' there wunt nothin' to be done up our way, they all drifted back down to Massachusetts, where a few days later they held a memorial service for the dear departed. On account of the circumstances of her departure there was no need to order a casket; prob'ly a considerable savings to the family right there.

I suppose the whole thing was pretty tough on the family, but fortunately life goes on. A couple of weeks later the whole incident had pretty well blowed over and things was gettin' back to normal. Bert and I was down to the fisherman's co-op on Friday mornin' about 5:00. I was finishin' my second cup of coffee and Bert was over in the corner playin' the Pac Man machine when Richard Wall, one of the local lobstermen, come over and started in with a little friendly banter.

"You remember that heavyset girl you boys had out fishin' with y' a couple weeks back?" he says.

"Ayuh," I replied.

"Well," he went on, "I just thought I'd let y' know she

SHE HAD AN EXTREMELY LARGE HEART!
AMONGST OTHER THINGS!

washed up on the beach down to Mill Cove last night."

"Y' don't say!"

"Ayuh, musta been the same one. 'Bout the size of a pilot whale?"

"That's her all right," I muttered. "What kinda shape was she in?"

"Not too shabby," he said, "considerin' where she's been and all. I will say she had almost two dozen good-sized lobsters clingin' to 'er."

"Y' don't say," I replied.

"Ayuh," said Richard. "Most of 'em 'd run two pounds or better."

I thanked him for the information and went across the room to break the news to Bert.

"Godfrey," he exclaimed, lookin' visibly upset. "They've already had the service and everything. What am I gonna do now?"

"Look, Bert," I said. "I realize this is kinda touchy. It's really a family matter, and I prob'ly ought to stay out of it altogether. But things bein' as they are, what with the state of the economy and the price of lobsters and so forth. . . . Well, my advice would be *set 'er again!*"